MAKE MORE
THAN YOUR PARENTS

MAKE MORE
THAN YOUR PARENTS

YOUR GUIDE TO FINANCIAL FREEDOM

MIKE BUNDLIE – KEVIN O'DONNELL – DR. BART DILIDDO

www.gotmoola.com

Health Communications, Inc.
Deerfield Beach, Florida

www.hcibooks.com

Library of Congress Cataloging-in-Publication Data

Bundlie, Mike, date.
  Make more than your parents : your guide to financial freedom / Mike Bundlie,
Kevin O'Donnell, Bart Diliddo.
    p. cm.
  ISBN 0-7573-0122-3 (tp)
  1. Finance, Personal. 2. Saving and investment. 3. Investments.
  I. O'Donnell, Kevin, date. II. Diliddo, Bart, date. III. Title.

HG179.B824 2003
332.024'01—dc21

2003056556

Publisher: Health Communications, Inc.
              3201 S.W. 15th Street
              Deerfield Beach, Florida 33442-8190

This book is dedicated to the family and friends of all future entrepreneurs and innovators. Their support and patience are the building blocks on which Financial Freedom is built.

Mike Bundlie, Kevin O'Donnell, and Dr. Bart DiLiddo

PUBLISHED BY
Health Communications, Inc.
The Life Issues Publisher

CONTRIBUTING WRITERS
Heidi Fargo Bundlie
Mary Louise Hamilton

PRODUCTION EDITOR
Heidi Fargo Bundlie
Linda Royer

PROOFREADING
Beth Hoffman
Patricia Martin

LAYOUT / ILLUSTRATION / COVER
Mike Bundlie

MAIN SECTIONS

EARNING MONEY

Making money is what this book is all about. Find out how to get a job or start your own company.

SPENDING MONEY

When you've got it, you spend it. Find out how to spend it wisely, while having fun along the way.

SAVING MONEY

A big step in reaching your goal. Find out the exciting ways you can take charge of where your money goes.

INVESTING MONEY

Time to step up and make your money work for you. Find out how to make your money grow.

TABLE OF CONTENTS

QUICK BOOK GUIDE

JUMP ONLINE
gotmoola.com

This book is just the beginning. This symbol points out places where the web site can further your adventure.

TIPS AND TRICKS

A banana a day is a good idea. So is reading the helpful tips and tricks that you'll find when you see this symbol.

WRITE AWAY

You can write anywhere in this book but the sections with this symbol give you some good ideas about what to write.

write on me

CHAPTER 1

GETTING STARTED

SO YOU WANT TO MAKE MORE THAN YOUR PARENTS?

Good! You should! Prices rise every day. Making money is hard work, but it is also fun. We'll show you how to turn it into a game. It is even more fun when the money you make starts to make more money for you through smart investments. No matter how young you are, you're old enough to get started. The fact that you are reading this book means that you have an interest in making money. That interest, combined with focus, consistent work, and a zest for learning, will result in you having tremendous financial resources.

Many people spend their whole lives struggling with money because they don't understand how to keep enough of what they make. The more money you put to work for you, the more money you will have.

FINANCIAL FREEDOM?

The biggest goal of this book is to show you how to achieve the grand prize of **Financial Freedom**. There will be smaller goals on the way, but they should all lead to winning this great prize. But what is it?

Financial Freedom means you can live just as you like without having to worry about money. Many people think the goal is to get rich. However, if you still need to make more money to pay for everything you own, you do not have financial freedom and you will be stressed!

That's why so many rich people aren't really happy. But, given the chance, it's probably better to be rich and stressed than poor and stressed. In either case we're going to show you how to make as much money as you'd like and turn it into much more than you could ever imagine. You could even make more than your parents.

If you go to **gotmoola.com**, you can play money games online with Moola the Monkey. Reading this book will help you win.

When you see the symbol to the left, it means that there's a cool tip on that page that relates to the web site.

There are opportunities all around you to earn money using your imagination, talent and willingness to work hard. This book will help you take advantage of these opportunities and gain an ever-growing portfolio of assets. Your portfolio will ultimately reach a point where the assets produce more money each year than you need to live.

At this point you win! You have Financial Freedom. That's the game, that's how you win… The only thing left to do is to learn how to play, and that's what the rest of this book is about.

WE SUGGEST FIVE CATEGORIES TO SET AS YOUR GOALS:

- **STUFF** (Clothes, Video Games, Toys, Movies, etc.)
- **GEAR** (Moped, Bike, Car, Cell Phone, Computer, etc.)
- **EDUCATION** (College, Trade School, Lessons, Camp, etc.)
- **BIZ** (Start a Business, Open a Recording Studio, etc.)
- **CRIB** (Buy your own home)

Keep these goals in mind as you read. A good way to think about them is as the prizes you will earn as you get better at the game of making money. **Remember, the more you enjoy it, the better you'll do!** This book is something to have fun with and to take your time with. You can jump around or stay on a chapter for two weeks if you want. Bounce back and forth between the Internet and this book. Use it in whatever way works for you. It's your book. In the upcoming chapters there are a lot of fun things to do.

Part of what we want you to do is to let yourself have really big ideas; ideas that are too big for the boxes that most people's brains put ideas in. Your ideas will be so big that they need to go "outside the box."

Some people in life try very hard to look and act like other people. It is okay to emulate good behavior and bold thinking, but never settle for anything less than the real you. What makes you most unique and valuable is that different twist in the way you see things. Be proud of your individuality. This book, along with the web site will show you how to use your unique qualities and gifts to gain **Financial Freedom**.

Have a blast! There are opportunities all around you...

The scorecard for the game of making money is called your **portfolio**.

One of the first things you'll be doing is setting up your own portfolio to keep track of how you are doing.

A portfolio is like a big wallet that includes all of the different accounts that you will be setting up. We will show you which types of accounts to put in your portfolio and will talk about how to do it. We will also help you figure out how to make these funds grow via your investments and the new dollars you earn. Don't worry if your portfolio looks small at the beginning. It's like a seed just waiting to grow up big and strong.

One of the great things about this game is that the more you cooperate with everyone else playing, the more money you make. This is the wonder of the economy and the creativity of life. You can think up ideas and create your own job or start with a job from someone else.

This is part of the game of life and the more you play, the more you win. Use your wits, personality and determination to achieve great things in life. When someone creates a company that employs thousands of people, they are helping all of those people have better lives. That can be you!

The biggest prize we want you to think about for now is your **Educational Fund**. Your personal path may have you taking college courses via satellite from a remote village in Africa where you are helping with the Peace Corps. Or you may find yourself on an Ivy League Campus with other bright, determined, upbeat people in an environment centered around learning and discovery. You can go to college; no matter how much money you or your parents have right now. It just means setting that as a goal for you to win.

One of the keys to winning is starting to play early. Now! That's right. You've already started by opening this book. **Congratulations!** You are starting young and because of this you have a huge advantage in the game. You have time as your ally.

Many people will tell you that because you are young you should take big risks. When it comes to the way you save and invest your money, we're telling you the exact opposite. Because you are young you have time to allow safe investments to grow. Use your age as a key weapon. Always make sure your money is safe.

SOME SWEET DREAMIN'

If money didn't matter, what would you do as your ideal job? Write it here. Don't worry if it seems silly. What is it about that job that makes it sound fun?

_____

_____

_____

_____

_____

YOUR DREAMS, YOUR LIFE

Remember, **Financial Freedom** is the grand prize that you are playing for. We want you to write your goals down because Financial Freedom is the moment that you can do what you want to do, and still have enough money to pay for your life.

Before we're done, you are going to have ideas for your own business. You're going to have your own **portfolio**, with investments growing inside of it for you. You are going to know lots of tricks for finding work and getting money. You are also going to read about other young people who have made money. Some of them are already millionaires! You are also going to discover how much fun it is to make and save money.

Think of it this way… say that right now you have fun playing basketball. How much fun would it be to own a basketball team? Here's a person that did just that. Mark Cuban started his first business when he was fourteen years old, and now owns the Dallas Mavericks basketball team. We asked Mark what advice he would give someone your age, and this is what he wanted us to tell you…

"Do what you love to do, and have the most fun with... Work hard to do it better than anyone else, and great things can happen... your dreams can come true!"

Mark has his own basketball team, his own high-definition television network and parts of many other businesses. He flies around the world on his jet and does whatever he wants. Guess what? He started when he was your age with no more than what you have right now. Probably less. He plays the money game really well.

Do what you love to do and do it better than anyone else. You will naturally work harder when you enjoy what you are doing.

What you do with your money is up to you. Hopefully, you will use it to do good in your life and in the lives of others. Money is neither good nor bad; it's just one way of keeping score in the game of life.

We want you to win! In this book you are going to play a lot of games that will sharpen your mind and prepare you to go out into the real world as a winner! You have a secret ally in this book. Keep it close, take your time reading it, and follow the advice inside. Most importantly, have fun!

One of the people that wanted to make sure this information was available to you is a wise man by the name of Dr. Bart DiLiddo. Bart has spent a great deal of his life studying investments and he has helped a lot of people achieve **Financial Freedom**. He will help you too. We asked Bart to write you a letter that has financial secrets in it.

Picky, Picky...

Read the following letter and pick the three words you think are most important for someone who wants to grow up with financial freedom.

Out of these, see if you select the same words that our experts chose as the top three. Our answers are written upside down at the end of the letter.

When I was a boy, I made a wish. This wish was so important to me that I was willing to put every ounce of energy I had into making it come true. I wished I could earn one cent a minute. Yes, sixty cents an hour! If I could make sixty cents an hour, all my money problems would be solved. It would be wonderful.

In this day and age, sixty cents an hour may not sound like very much, but it was a king's ransom to a nine year-old, making 10 cents an hour shining shoes in 1940. It was more money than my dad was making.

So I shined shoes, stocked shelves, set pins, delivered the morning paper, washed walls, cut grass, shoveled snow, ran errands, and caddied to earn whatever money I could.

Finally, when I was seventeen, I achieved my goal of making sixty cents an hour as a caddy. I caddied every day except Monday to make about $30.00 a week.

Out of this, I made a very important decision... I wasn't going to spend the rest of my life doing manual labor. I was going to college. I graduated from three different colleges, received a Ph.D. in Chemical Engineering from Case Institute of Technology and, as a Senior Executive, attended Harvard Business School and the Sloan School of Management at MIT. Because I worked and received financial aid, my folks didn't have to spend a single cent on me for books or tuition.

While all of this sounds pretty serious, I actually had a lot of fun during my school years. I played sports, dated, and was president of my high school class and college fraternity. Although I wasn't an angel and made mistakes, I never deliberately did anything that would bring shame to me or my family.

The best investment I ever made was in going to college. It allowed me to be successful beyond my wildest dreams. You can do the same. We live in a great country. Opportunity is all around us. Work hard, have fun and stay out of trouble.

– Dr. Bart DiLiddo

Key words: energy, goal, college

By the way, it doesn't matter if you don't have money right now. You can be living in a tough situation and still start building your own financial foundation.

 You can go online at school or the library and hook into a network of mentors, scholarships and opportunities we've set up for you at *gotmoola.com*. If you want to make money, you can do it through fair, positive means that bring friends and adventures to you throughout your life.

Anyone can do it. It takes effort! You just saw that Bart did it. You can do it, too. You're going to win big time if you play by the rules in this book. **Financial Freedom** here you come! You are going to be a leader. So think big. Think fun. Think responsibly. Most of all… think!

> "I always wanted to be somebody,
> but I should have been more specific."
> – Lily Tomlin

Now, let's take a deeper look at why it's so important to make more than your parents. Ask your parents how much an apartment or house like yours cost when they were your age. You'll discover that it cost a lot less money than it does now. **YOU HAVE TO MAKE MORE THAN YOUR PARENTS**, just to live at the same level that you and your parents are living at now. Don't worry if it seems impossible. You'll be amazed at how the impossible can become possible. It happens one step at a time. By seeing how much they had at your age, you can start playing the game with this as one of your benchmarks. It will help you in the game and it will be fun.

The good news is that there are more ways than ever before to make money. It doesn't take a genius. It just takes determination.

HOW MUCH WAS IT?

IN MY DAY...

Ask your parents how much the items below cost when they were your age. Write down the prices in the second column. Then, write down the cost of the same items today in the third column. If you don't know what the item costs, ask your parents or a friend.

ITEM	$ THEN	$ NOW
Candy bar		
Movie		
Bike		
TV		
Car		
College		
House		

Genius is 1 percent inspiration and 99 percent perspiration.

– Thomas Edison

HOW MUCH IS MONEY WORTH?

Benjamin Franklin said that if you want to know how much money is worth, try and borrow some from someone. Try it. Your parents or a generous aunt might give you a few dollars if you ask them for it, but they'll look at you like you're crazy if you ask for hundreds or thousands of dollars.

YOU'RE NOT ALONE

Even though your financial future is your responsibility, you're not alone. All around you are people that can help you make more money. The most important resources you have are the people that you know. Your family, your friends, your teachers - all of them can help. It's up to you to figure out how. Then there are people that you may not have met that can help: your banker, your investment counselor, your broker – yes, you can have a broker even at your age.

Go online to **gotmoola.com** to learn more. These people get paid by their companies to help you make more money, so don't be afraid to talk to them. We'll discuss what each of these people can do for you later in the book.

People Resources...

Think about the people you know. All of them are resources, people resources. A resource is any asset, connection, material or knowledge that you can draw upon to use or create something.

These people might be able to help you directly, by driving you around or lending you money. People can also help you indirectly by giving their opinion about an idea you've had or by encouraging you to try harder. Keeping track of how people can help you gives you more flexibility as you find ways to make more money.

Make a list of your current resources. Write down people that you interact with on a regular basis and their relationship to you. Continue adding to this list as you meet new people. Start with your family. If you need a place to write, go to the back of the book. Have fun!

You'll be surprised at how excited some of these people will be to help a motivated, sharp young person like yourself get started on the road to financial freedom. So don't be shy. For all they know, you're going to be one of the richest people in the world when you get older.

Guess what, you may just be, though that's not the key here. We want you to understand money so that no matter what you want to do in life, you have the financial ability to achieve it. Here is a young man who had a dream and started a company that you may know about.

GUESS WHO...

Read the mystery bio below and see if you can guess what famous person we're talking about.

A young animator went to New York to speak with the people that sold his cartoons to movie theaters. His cartoons were popular, and theaters liked to play them before the regular movies. The young animator was hoping to raise his price. However, when he arrived, he was told that the company would no longer be buying the cartoon from him. Even worse, they used a clause in their contract to take over the rights to the cartoon. Even worse than that, they had already hired some of his best artists to come work for them.

The young animator left the meeting feeling devastated. He'd just lost his contract, cartoon and best artists. He didn't have the heart to tell his brother—who was his partner—the bad news. Instead he sent him a message that everything was good and that he'd be back in California in a few days, with all of the details. He took a train back and decided that he couldn't give up and he started drawing. By the time the train rolled into Los Angeles, the young animator had a brand new cartoon character that ended up being very successful.

Can you guess who we're talking about?

That animator was Walt Disney, and the character was Mickey Mouse™.

Evan & Elise Macmillan

- Company: ChocolateFarm.com™
- Biz Whiz @ Age: 13 & 10

WHAT THEY DID:

- Turned their interests into a successful product
- Stayed focused

When he was thirteen years old, Evan Macmillan was already on his way to financial freedom. He had an account at a great bank called the Young Americans Bank in Denver, Colorado that was just for kids. Evan knew that his little sister, Elise, really liked to make chocolates and they both liked animals, so they decided to make handmade farm-themed chocolates.

Together, they submitted a one-page business plan to be part of an event at their bank. It was only going to be a one-day project, but Evan made a Web site, *www.chocolatefarm.com*, and soon, they were getting thousands of orders. They were getting so many orders that they couldn't make their candy at home anymore. Their parents gave them the money to make the Chocolate Farm into a real business. With their help and a $5,000 loan from their bank they could afford to use a big commercial kitchen and hire some people to work for them.

Now they have forty part-time employees, a successful Web site, a cookbook, and chocolate kits so people can make their own Chocolate Farm candy at home. Evan says that "It is relatively easy to make a list of things you are good at and love to do. It is harder to focus this interest and learn everything you can about it with the goal of starting a business."

Paige Courtney Dunn

- Company: LeftGear.com™
- San Francisco, California

WHAT SHE DID:

- Recognized an underserved market
- Used her interests for success

Paige started modeling when she was ten and was a finalist for *Seventeen*'s cover model contest when she was fifteen. Her picture has been on magazine covers, but she left all that behind to get her education. Paige graduated from the University of California, Berkeley and the American Conservatory Theatre School in San Francisco. When she was twenty-six, she started *LeftGear.com*, a website that sells products by forty of LA's best young designers.

Paige saw an opportunity to use the Internet to start her own store without having to pay for the building. She also knew a lot about fashion and clothing and had met many of the top new designers. Paige knew she had to learn as much as possible before starting Left Gear so she did a lot of research. Her dad was also a big help—she called him almost every day! When Paige started to sell clothes online, she knew how to present and promote them so people would want to buy them. Because she started modeling so young, Paige grew up thinking about money and business. Her parents let her use her money how she wanted. That early experience with success helped Paige learn how to handle money. Paige knew she was taking a big risk starting her own company. However, because of all the work she had down in the industry, she was prepared for success.

PORTFOLIO TIME

A key word for you to keep in mind is **EDUCATION!**

Did you notice that Paige got her idea from the things that she loved? She recognized a need and then sought out the knowledge necessary to address that need, through education. Education is not restricted to school, though. Paige's modeling was an important part of her education as it taught her about the market and introduced her to the resources she would need to start her business. Reading this book is part of your education. Speaking with your mom or dad about their job or spending the day there is part of your education.

Get as much education as you can because it is a key part of the fuel you will need to make it to your final destination. That destination is your ultimate goal: **Financial Freedom**. Never stop your education. Go to college. It's a lot of fun and you can study just about anything there. In order to do that, you're going to need to have an education fund in your portfolio.

YOUR FIRST PORTFOLIO

Remember, your portfolio is like your big wallet. A portfolio holds all of your saved **assets**. These may be stocks, a savings account, a coin collection, a savings bond, a valuable trading card or an antique doll collection. Your portfolio is a list of all these things. Next to each asset is the amount of money that they are worth. Your portfolio should be updated every week and it should be in a place that you can update it whenever you want to.

You can go to *gotmoola.com* and learn more about making your first portfolio. You are worth more than you think.

HOW MUCH MONEY DO YOU HAVE?

$ VALUE

	$ VALUE
Cash:	
Bank Accounts:	
Stock Accounts:	
Savings Bonds:	
Value of your stuff:	
Gifts / Trusts:	
Other:	
TOTAL:	

Ask your parents how much money they had in their portfolio when they were your age. They'll be impressed that you used the word "portfolio."

POSITIVE ATTITUDE

Set your mind to making money and you will succeed at it. Right now, you have no idea how much money you will make in your life, so don't put any limitations on it. Get into the habit of building a positive image about money. Every day repeat this simple saying to yourself:

"I am a person who sees opportunity, attracts money, has fun making it and invests it wisely. I will gain financial freedom."

This may seem like a silly thing to do, but the results may impress you. Thoughts are things, put them to use for you. Think good thoughts and good things will happen. Say this daily for one year and just see what happens. You may be surprised.

LET'S SET UP AN ACCOUNT

The first thing you will want to do is set up your **education fund**. You'll need to have a bank account to begin. Let's walk through setting up your first account.

Start Your Engines...

STEP 1
Stop in to your local bank and introduce yourself to one of the bankers. Don't worry if you don't have any money right now. Ask them what kind of college savings programs they offer people your age. You might get a better deal than your parents! If you already have a savings account, you're ahead of the game. Speak with your parents about it.

STEP 2

Ask the banker how you can open a savings account and an education fund. Find out what the interest rates are on the accounts.

Lastly, find out if there is a minimum balance that you need to have in the accounts each month. Bring this book with you and write the amounts that they say below.

A parent may need to accompany you the first time or two on trips to the bank when you actually start the account. It's not hard. You can use funds already available in your existing portfolio or you can earn new dollars. There are lots of ways to earn new dollars coming up.

| Minimum Balance:
Interest Rate:

Goal 1: Date opened

Goal 2: Amount that you
will put in each month | |

STEP 3
Your education fund is the first priority in your portfolio so we want to give you a tip on how to make it grow. Once you have set up an account with either your local bank or online, you need to plan how to put money into it.

One of the best ways is to make a deal with your parents. Tell them that college is a big dream of yours and that each month you are going to put $20 into your account. Ask them to match it. Your parents will like that you are helping pay for your education and it shows that you are willing to work for it. Suddenly, you are getting twice as much money and your account is growing faster than it would otherwise.

In the first year alone you will put $480 into this account and with interest you could have well over $500 at the end of the year. You can also suggest to your parents that they sign up for automatic deposits with the bank, so that the money goes into your account every month automatically. **YOU'RE ON YOUR WAY!**

Now that you have a portfolio, there are a lot of ways to build it up. The bigger it is, the better you're doing! To really do it successfully you'll need to know the secrets behind the four basics of money: **EARNING**, **SPENDING**, **SAVING**, and **INVESTING**. In the next four chapters we'll go over ways to make money work for you! That's right. The more knowledge you have about how money works, the better you'll be at making more. *LET'S LOOK AT EARNING MONEY FIRST...*

CHAPTER 2

EARNING MONEY

Now that you know how much money you have in your portfolio, and you know how much you need for your college fund the next step is earning money. In 2001, teens in the U.S. earned over $200 billion. That's a lot of money! Finding ways to earn money can be fun and very rewarding. All it takes is a little creativity and the desire to make it happen. Think you've got what it takes? You do. All you have to do is start.

There are an infinite number of ways to earn money. In fact, the people that have earned the most money are often the people that have found their own unique way of doing it.

FIRST TIME OUT...

Guess how much money your mom or dad or grandma or grandpa made in their first job.

Guess what they did and guess how much money they got paid for every week they worked. Then, go ask them and compare your answers.

How old were they?

What did they do?

How much money did they make each week?

As you go out and begin earning your own money, keep looking for even better ways of earning, and you'll soon see your money growing faster and faster. Let's look at a couple ways that you can get started earning money.

EMPLOYMENT

At some point your parents have probably said or will probably say something like, "If you want more money, why don't you get a job?!" For most people, getting a job is the fastest way to guarantee that they will make money. **That's because a job is basically a trade.**

You trade your services to a person or company willing to give you an agreed upon amount of money, a wage, for those services. That person or company is referred to as the employer and you are referred to as an employee. How much money you make depends greatly on the type of job you choose and how valuable the service is to the employer.

The good news is that there are endless varieties of jobs as well as a few good tricks to keep in mind when you want to get one.

TIP: Your parents and friends can be a good source for finding jobs.

TRICKS FOR GETTING EMPLOYED:

1 – Be creative. Look around you. See who you know that needs help. This could be a company that you often visit, a neighbor or a family member. Knowing that someone needs your services helps you negotiate the best wage. There may be a person on the block who would love to hire you to fix things in his/her home or a business person that travels a lot and would find it worthwhile to have their trash cans taken out and put back each week. Look at people and think about what would make their life easier or better and then think of ways you could do that for them.

23

Frank Epperson

- Invention: Popsicles™
- Biz Whiz @ Age: 11

WHAT HE DID:

- Identified a new market
- Combined his interests with accidental invention

Frank Epperson was eleven years old when he accidentally "invented" the Popsicle.

Frank had mixed some soda water powder and water one afternoon, which was a popular drink in those days. He left the mixture on the back porch overnight with the stirring stick still in it. The temperature dropped to a record low that night and the next day Frank had a stick of frozen soda water to show his friends at school.

In 1923, eighteen years later, Frank Epperson remembered his frozen soda water mixture and began a business producing Epsicles in seven fruit flavors. The name was later changed to the Popsicle™. It is estimated that 3 million Popsicle frozen treats are sold each year.

Today there are more than thirty different flavors to choose from, but Popsicle Industries says the hottest flavor through the years has remained "taste-tingling orange."

Michael Furdyk

- Company: MyDesktop.com™
- Biz Whiz @ Age: 16

WHAT HE DID:

- Recognized an underserved market
- Followed his interests

When he was a kid, Michael Furdyk wanted to be an astronaut, but it was his interest in computers that made him a millionaire. Michael sold his first company for more than $1 million before his eighteenth birthday, how did he do it? Along with two of his friends, Michael started *MyDesktop.com*, a computer community made up of several web sites and email newsletters.

His interest in computers helped Michael start a company that provided a unique service to his customers. His websites allowed people to interact with people in up to 200 other countries. Michael took his success and his skills with computers one step further when he started *TakingITGlobal.org* when he was seventeen.

With *TakingITGlobal*, Michael helps other young people get involved in projects to help them realize their potential. Michael spends five to seven hours online every day, checking his email and making his websites better and easier to use. He likes to keep himself informed about issues other than computers, though. He cares about the environment and is interested in finding new ways to spread information around the globe and maybe even beyond. Michael may not be an astronaut, but that hasn't stopped him from reaching for the stars.

BIZ WHIZ

Roubbins Jamal LaMothe

- Writer, Artist, Achiever
- Biz Whiz @ Age: 18

WHAT HE DID:

- Believed in his abilities
- Found an avenue for sharing his thoughts and ideas

Roubbins LaMothe was eighteen when he published his first book, *Lessons I Have Learned: The Autobiography of Roubbins LaMothe*. The book was only twenty pages long, but for Roubbins it wasn't about writing the longest or best-selling book in the country. For Roubbins, it was about self-confidence. When he heard some of his friends talking about publishing their own books, Roubbins was skeptical. Not believing they could publish books, he went to see what they were talking about. He found out that they were involved with Books of Hope, a program started by a woman named Anika Nailah to show kids without many resources that they could do anything if they tried. Roubbins has published 9 books in less than four years. Writing about his own experiences has been rewarding for Roubbins. He has found out that people want to read about the truth, not just about happy endings.

Now, Roubbins is studying to become a social worker. He's also working on a documentary film. For Roubbins, the most important thing is informing other people about the world around them. He believes that his books and films will inspire others to create something important too.

2 – Network. Network. Network. Asking around can open many doors for you. The people in your life may know about job opportunities that you haven't thought of yet. They also can be excellent sources of positive referrals for your new employer. You simply start by asking people you know if they know of any work for someone your age. Remember, this is not rocket science. Just ask the question: "Excuse me, but do you happen to know of anyone looking for someone to do part-time work?" That's it. Just say those words to people you know and you will start to have opportunities placed in front of you. Remember... you are a person who sees opportunities in all directions, attracts money, has fun making it and invests it wisely so that you can live financially free.

Think Big – Start Small – Don't Give Up

3 – Do some footwork. Sometimes you just have to do a bit of research. Go to your favorite mall with a couple friends and look to see who is hiring. Ask the sales people if their store is hiring. Also ask them if the manager is a good boss. Ask if it is a good place to work. Always think about your choices and choose the best option. If the employees of one store like their work and the other store's employees don't, well... which one are you going to choose? Footwork means gathering intelligence. Think of yourself as a detective, going out collecting information that will allow you to make key strategic decisions about how to earn money.

4 – If there is a place that you like to go, such as a clothing store or a skateboard park, introduce yourself to the person in charge and tell them that you'd be willing to help out if they need it. If you do this for a few days it is very likely that they will then offer you a job once they see that you have a good attitude and are reliable.

EARNING MONEY:

A TRUE LITTLE TALE

A fourteen-year-old dancer in California found herself repeatedly in the Dance Supply Shop next to the studio at which she took numerous dance classes. She started answering customers' questions one day when the small sales staff was busy. Soon, she started helping out and selling outfits for fun. Soon thereafter, she was hired to work two hours per week in one shift that fell between two of her classes and matched the time that the shop owner needed help.

In this case, the girl applied for the job by showing she was a valuable asset. She had the ability to sell clothes and act responsibly in the store environment. **She was valuable.**

Let's look at the steps that she took to get her job and start earning money. Following this path applies to many different types of jobs. Think about how to achieve these steps for your ideal job.

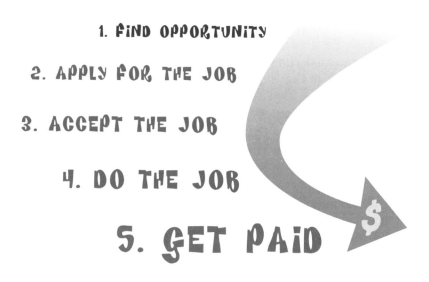

1. FIND OPPORTUNITY

2. APPLY FOR THE JOB

3. ACCEPT THE JOB

4. DO THE JOB

5. GET PAID

APPLYING FOR A JOB

Applying for a job is as simple as asking your next-door neighbor for two dollars to wash their car... or dog. It's also as complicated as filling out a form and doing a formal interview with a person running a business. In either case there are simple rules to keep in mind.

Wear clean clothes, be polite, be truthful and pay attention.

Keep in mind that you are a valuable, unique individual with the capacity to execute numerous procedures simultaneously.

> **TRANSLATION:** You can talk and write back and forth with friends while doing your homework and watching part of a show on TV. You can multi-task **AND** you can focus and do what someone asks of you. You are valuable. There are many jobs, find the one that is right for you.

Many bosses will tell you that the hardest thing to find is a good, punctual, polite, bright, responsible employee. You can be all of those things. You just need to decide to act this way at work. If you do this, you will be a valuable employee.

It will also lead sooner to the day that you are the boss. Later on we'll show you how to set up a company. It's fun. You can be your own boss! Good concept. Think about it. You can do it.

EARNING MONEY:

There may be a place that you think would be fun to work at, but it's not the type of place where you can just offer to help out. In this case, you are going to need to apply to be an employee. Before you do, follow these steps…

- Think about why you want to work there.

- How many hours each day or week can you work?

- How much do you think you should be paid?

- Is this job going to be in a safe, positive environment?

- Discuss the job with your parents.

If you want a job, ask for it proudly, and with the thought of how you are going to use part of this money to build your portfolio. The other part you can use to get things you want. You have financial resources. You are a consumer. **You are part of the economy.** Your future is bright and filled with promise. Get your education and as you do so, build your portfolio. Learn and earn! And have fun along the way. Once you start working for a real company, you will begin to pay money in taxes. Some of these taxes are going right into a bank account for you that will be part of your portfolio for the rest of your life.

You deserve to be in the best situation possible.

FOR EXAMPLE: If there are two fast-food restaurants nearby, take an hour and observe them both for a half-hour and see which one is run better, is cleaner, and has more of the people working there smiling. That's a better place to work.

CREATING A RESUME

A resume is a one-page sheet with your name and contact information on the top. Below this, you list personal information that may be of interest or value to a potential employer. You are selling **you** to the employer. Highlight the positive things about what you can do, as well as your goals. People interviewing you will respond positively to this.

Below is an example of a good starting resume. You can create your own resume at **gotmoola.com**

Kevin Tuckahoohoo
Phone: 200-555-8921
Email: info@gotmoola.com

EDUCATION:
Junior at Tiller High School

ORGANIZATIONS:
Yearbook Club, Junior Varsity Baseball Team

TALENTS:
Hip Hop DJ, Piano

JOB EXPERIENCE:
Weekly landscape and upkeep for neighbors, Baby-sitting, Cart Assistant at local fair

HOBBIES:
Hiking, Inventing things, Sketching

GOALS:
To Graduate from high school with good grades and to go to college to study business while I build my career as a DJ. To find a worthwhile, positive job experience that can help me build my college fund while at the same time helping me understand how a business operates.

SENDING OUT YOUR RESUME

When you walk into a company you want to work for, have a resume with you. Leave one behind with whomever you speak to. You may need to pass out fifty resumes before you get a job. That's fine.

You can also email your resume to companies, or mail it. If you mail it, address it to the place of business in care of the hiring person's name (if you know it). If not, then mail it to the company with "ATTN: PERSONNEL" written underneath the company name.

THE INTERVIEW

When you go in for an interview of any sort, do the following:

- Make sure your parents know where you are going, when and why.

- Walk in five minutes early and politely ask for the person you need to see.

- Be patient and treat everyone there with respect.

When you are interviewed, it simply means that someone will speak with you for a few moments and ask you questions. Answer the questions truthfully and confidently. In your mind, reverse the process and pretend that you are the one doing the interviewing. After all, if you don't like this person you won't want to hire them on as your boss. Listen to what they say and make sure you ask questions about just what would be expected of you. Remember, you are responsible. You are bright. You are honest. You can multi-task. They need you. If this isn't the right person or company to work for, then move on!

ACCEPTING A JOB

When someone offers you a job, and someone will, you need to settle upon a wage you will be paid for the work you do. This is typically an hourly amount. Many places that you will have access to will offer **minimum wage**.

This is the minimum amount that the government demands businesses pay to employees. Out of this amount you will have Social Security deducted from your paycheck as well as applicable State and Federal taxes.

Even though you may not think there is a chance for more money than they offer, ask. Say these words:

> "Thank you for your offer, is it possible to boost the rate up ten percent? If I don't prove to you that I'm worth it, feel free to cut it back to your original offer before you pay me my first paycheck." **Always negotiate.**

Ask for what you believe is fair, and don't settle for something you feel is unfair, just say, "No Thank You" and leave. When you do accept an offer, seal it with a handshake as you repeat back the terms one more time so that you both understand the terms of your agreement. When you get home, write the terms down and, if possible, review them with your parents.

DOING THE JOB

OK, now you have the job! There are two types of employees. Those who simply put in their time and can't wait to get off work, and those who look at each day at work as another day of learning. The former may do okay, but the latter will climb the ladder, quickly.

EARNING MONEY:

GETTING PAID

When you get paid, **SMILE!** You just earned money. Now, be very smart with your money. Before you spend any of it, first look at your portfolio. How much of your paycheck can you put into your portfolio? At your age, the minimum amount that you should put in is 25 percent. Some very aggressive people your age may put 75 percent or more of it away. Set your priorities and then stick to them. Your portfolio will end up having more than one account so you will have to determine where your money goes each month. You can even set it up online so that your paychecks are automatically deposited by your employer into your accounts. This is called **direct deposit**.

Be smart with your paycheck. This is your money.

Your paycheck came to you only after you worked hard for it. When you put part of that paycheck into your portfolio, it starts to work for you. You start making money just by keeping your money in an investment. Now you're making money at work, and you're also making money in your portfolio. This is how people get rich. They make more than they spend and they invest the money they keep wisely.

TEN TIPS TO SUCCEEDING IN YOUR JOB

1 – BE ON TIME

2 – DRESS PROPERLY

3 – HAVE GOOD PERSONAL HYGIENE

4 – BE POLITE

5 – STAY FOCUSED ON YOUR WORK

6 – LOOK FOR WAYS TO HELP

7 – ADMIT YOUR MISTAKES

8 – BE HONEST

9 – BE POSITIVE

10 – KEEP LEARNING

Follow these tips and your responsibility as well as your paycheck will grow and grow!

35

SOCIAL SECURITY

Most places will require that you have a Social Security number before they can hire you. **Social Security** is the name of a huge portfolio of tax money that Americans and American companies pay into through payroll deductions. When someone reaches retirement age, they will then get money back from the Social Security portfolio for the rest of their lives. If you are an employee of a company, you will need to provide them with your Social Security number. Then the taxes they take out of your paycheck will be credited to your Social Security account.

Congratulations, you're a taxpayer! Once you turn fourteen you can file your own tax return. If your parents agree and do it with you, it will be a very good thing for you to start doing. It isn't hard. Your parents should have already obtained your Social Security number.

Whenever you work for someone who takes Social Security taxes out of your pay, these taxes are credited to your account. If they don't take out taxes, you need to keep track of how much money you make. If you make over a certain amount every year you will need to report this money to the government, and pay the taxes on it yourself.

 If you have any unanswered questions, check with your parents or the people who employed you. We have also put links to useful employment resources online at *gotmoola.com*.

Remember, this isn't rocket science, anyone can do it. Just do things step by step. Though it may not seem so, time is on your side. Do the first thing and then the next and the next and you will eventually accomplish your goals.

TAXES

Understanding the basics of taxes is an important part of taking control of your financial future. It's really not as scary as it may seem. Just understand it and accurately keep track of all your financial transactions and you will never have a problem.

When you accumulate large amounts of money you will start looking more seriously at taxes and how to invest your money in ways that reduce the taxes on your earnings. However, keep in mind that taxes are what keep our country functioning effectively. If there were no taxes collected to pay the police, firefighters, or politicians, we would cease to exist as a functioning society. Paying taxes is a responsibility and an honor. It's part of being a good citizen.

There are four types of income tax that you need to be aware of:

1 – Federal Income Tax
In your first jobs, it is unlikely you will need to pay a federal income tax because there are minimum earnings that you must accumulate during the year before you are to be taxed. Employers may deduct taxes, but the government may send it back to you at the end of the year if you overpay your taxes. Your employer will remove a percentage of your earnings from each paycheck and send it into the U.S. Treasury. The less money you make, the lower percentage you pay. The federal income tax rate changes periodically whenever voters start telling their politicians they are paying too much money in taxes and will vote them out of office if they don't get a reduction.

2 – Social Security Tax
This is money for you down the road. One of the best parts of it is that whatever amount you put in is matched by your employer. It's a good deal for you.

3 – Medicare Tax

This is a small amount of tax taken by the Federal Government which is specifically directed into a fund to help pay for health care that is needed by people who have no other way to pay for it.

4 – State Income Tax

Most, but not all states, also take part of your earnings. The amount varies from state to state. This money goes into the State Fund and is used to pay for services not covered by the Federal Government.

It is important to know about taxes not only because not paying them is illegal, but also so that you have a better understanding of where the money goes when it is withheld from your paycheck.

To get a better idea of how much your paycheck will be each week, find out how much you might make per hour and how long you plan on working. Enter the information into the chart and start estimating how much will be taken out of your paycheck in taxes.

Just for fun, go to *www.irs.gov* and just click around. This is your service. Once you start paying taxes, you help pay for this site. This means it's partly yours. Use it. Don't be afraid of it. The more you understand about taxes, the smarter you will be with your portfolio.

You can also go online to calculate your taxes or see how long it will take you to earn your first $1 million dollars at different hourly rates. Check it out at *gotmoola.com*

CALCULATE YOUR PAYCHECK

WEEKLY EARNINGS   *TOTAL*

1 – Your hourly wage   _____

2 – Number of hours
     per week that you work   _____

3 – What you earn each week   _____
                                                     (#1 x #2)

TAXES WITHHELD   *YOU PAY*   *TOTAL*

4 – Federal Income Tax   ~ 15.0%   _____
                                             (#3 x .15)

5 – Social Security Tax   6.2%   _____
                                             (#3x .062)

6 – Medicare Tax   1.45%   _____
                                             (#3 x .0145)

7 – State Income Tax   ~ 5.0%   _____
                                             (#3 x .05)

8 – Total Taxes   _____
                                             (Add up #4 to #7)

YOUR PAYCHECK

9 – Remainder of Earnings   _____
                                             (#3 - #8)

CLIMBING THE LADDER

While being employed is a good way to start earning money, it has its limitations. In most jobs an increase in your wage, a raise, is decided by your employer and is statistically kept fairly low.

Let's say you are earning $500 per week, a 4 percent raise would bring you to $520 per week during the following year. Raises are not guaranteed, so you need to prove that you deserve one by the quality of your work.

Many smart people who choose employment as a way to earn money have made a career growth plan. This means that they have chosen a job that they enjoy and would like to get better at. As they get more experience they expect to change jobs within their company or with similar companies to higher paying positions.

A career growth plan can also be called a promotion plan. Each change of jobs to a higher paying position is called a promotion. It is important to remember that just like raises, promotions are not guaranteed. An example of a career growth plan is shown below.

Internship > Junior Level Employee > Senior Level Employee > Partner

There are other ways to make money besides working at a job in exchange for an annual or hourly rate. Albert Einstein started with a normal job as a clerk at a patent office. However, he soon went far beyond this to the point of thinker, inventor, spokesperson, activist, genius, speaker, and finally a teacher. Do you know what he says?

Imagination is more important than knowledge.
— Albert Einstein

IMAGINATION GAME

Write a word in the center of the space below and then write the next three words that come into your mind, all around it. The first word is something that you love. The next three are words that are connected in your mind with this thing you love to do…

Now around these three words write down five more words that relate. After you do this for each word, circle the ones that suggest ideas for jobs.

EARNING POTENTIAL

To increase your earnings faster you will need to take control of your **earning potential**.

Your earning potential is determined by how much you can realistically expect to earn in the future compared to what you currently earn. When another person or company determines your earnings they limit your earning potential.

If you invent something and sell it to people for more than it costs to make, your earning potential is huge. That's what people like Bill Gates of Microsoft and Stephen Jobs of Apple did.

Their earning potential is virtually unlimited. So is yours. You are starting to focus on your financial future. Understand that it will help you achieve more in life. You want to always think of ways to increase your earning potential.

In the case of employment, the raises that your company willing to give you limits your earning potential. The yearly average increase in wage is 4 percent. This means that your earning potential would also be 4 percent yearly. The fastest way to increase this amount is to look at other ways of earning money besides employment such as Sales, Invention, Entrepreneurship and Gifts.

What these methods all have in common is that you are in control of your earning potential. This means that with ingenuity and hard work you dramatically increase what you earn from year to year.

The downside to these methods is that they lack the security and stability of employment. You will need to decide what is more important to you.

Time to Be Bossy...

Start a make-believe company. What's your office like? Your business is growing and you need a personal assistant, for whom you are interviewing. You are interviewing for the position as both the boss and the employee. You are playing both parts.

To begin, place a mirror in your room and interview yourself. The real you is the boss, the mirror reflection is the employee applying for the job. Why do you want the job, why would you be good at it and how much can you work? Finally, how much money do you feel you should be paid?

Do it three times. The first time, settle for minimum wage. The next time, get an extra quarter per hour. The final time, go for a dollar more. It's fun. You'll find out you're a tough boss and a good person to hire. You'll also find out some things about yourself.

Double It...

Put a box under your bed. Put a dollar in it. One week later pull it out and put two more dollars in it. The next week pull it out and put four more dollars in it. A week later put in eight dollars and then sixteen the week after. Can you double it again, and again and again? When you finally can't double it anymore, invest it and start over. You'll start to get better at getting money.

The Back of a Buck...

Look at the back of a dollar bill and figure out what the symbols mean. Why is there a pyramid on the back of our money? Why is there an eye? Go to the library or the Internet, or ask a parent or teacher. See if you can find out what it all means by this time tomorrow.

Maria Montessori

Company: Montessori Schools™

Alcona, Italy

WHAT SHE DID:

- Identified a need
- Worked tirelessly to develop her idea

In 1870, when Maria Montessori was born in Italy, it was quite rare for a girl to get a college education. However, Maria wouldn't take no for an answer and in 1896 she graduated with a medical degree, becoming the first female doctor in Italy. She became fascinated with the way that little kids would start to play with things in her office and ask questions.

Maria decided to go back to college and learn more about how the human mind learns and develops. She went back to school because she believed that the way children were taught could be greatly improved. In 1906 she opened up a school where Maria developed a teaching style that allowed a child's natural curiosity to guide their education.

Maria's system quickly gained popularity in many countries. In 1913 she came to the United States and people as well known as Alexander Graham Bell, Thomas Edison and Helen Keller became supporters of hers. Today, there are thousands of Montessori schools everywhere from the United States to India. Prior to her death in 1952 Maria was nominated three times for the Nobel Peace Prize. Now, that is quite a teacher!

SALES & SERVICES – ENTREPRENEURS

Millions of people each year decide to become self-employed. Being self-employed means that you have chosen to be your own employer. **YOU ARE YOUR OWN BOSS!** The type of business that you will do is entirely up to you.

PICKING A PRODUCT

At the base of most self-employment scenarios is a product that you are selling. That is most often your labor and skill when you first start out. But it could just as easily be a product, like home made cookies. Choosing the right product to sell is as important as the sale itself. You don't want to sell ice at the North Pole. You need to make sure that there is going to be a market (demand for what you are going to sell). You also have to think about how to look at things. Here is an example of what we mean:

> A sunglass factory sends two marketing scouts to a remote region to study the prospects for expanding business. One sends back an email saying, **"SITUATION HOPELESS, NO ONE WEARS SUNGLASSES".** The other one writes back triumphantly, **"GLORIOUS BUSINESS OPPORTUNITY, THEY HAVE NO SUNGLASSES."**

There is opportunity all around you. You need to think about what's not there and how to get it there. When it comes to products, use yourself as a measure of demand. If you love a certain kind of cookie that your grandma makes, you might want to think about getting the recipe. Testing your product is a smart thing to do. Sometimes you may think of a product that doesn't even exist. Here's an example...

Thomas Adams

- Persistent, Opportunistic
- Gum!

WHAT HE DID:

- Recognized a new market
- Persisted despite setbacks

Thomas Adams tried a lot of different things before he came up with his road to riches. While working as a creative yet financially challenged photographer, in 1869, Thomas Adams learned of a Mexican tree product called "chicle."

Chicle had a rubbery texture and Thomas spent a year trying to turn it into tires, toys and even rain boots. However, none of his experiments worked. Finally, just when he was ready to throw the remaining chicle into a river, Thomas saw a girl buy a piece of paraffin based chewing gum for a penny. He knew that the indigenous people of Mexico had traditionally chewed chicle. He raced home with a new idea. Thomas and his sons cut the remaining chicle into little sticks and wrapped them in colored tissue paper. They took them back to the store and convinced the owner to try their new kind of gum. It was an instant hit and soon Thomas opened the world's first chewing gum factory.

When they started adding flavors to the chicle, their new product only became more popular. In 1888, one of the flavors, became the first gum to be sold in a vending machine.

EARNING MONEY:

PICKING A PRICE

Choosing the right price for your product can determine how hard the sale is going to be and how profitable you are going to be. There are different pricing philosophies that people use. The most common is called **keystoning**. This means doubling your price. Many clothing stores work this way.

When you see something being sold on TV with a phone number to call, you will be surprised to know, that of those items are sold for five times what they cost the person selling them to produce. This is because it is much harder to get someone to call from their home and buy something they see on TV than it is to get them to buy something when they are in a store. It is also because they probably got them very inexpensively because they bought a huge amount of them all at once and negotiated a very low price.

The more competition you have and the more expensive your product is to make, the lower your **profit** will be. Products that are unique or cheap to make often produce high profits.

The final determining factor of your pricing, however, is the price people will be willing to pay you for your product. In most cases **start by doubling** your cost and then adjust from there.

FINDING CLIENTS

One of the most challenging parts of sales is finding people to buy your product or service. Before you make a sale, people that you think would be good candidates are called leads. After they buy from you, they become customers or clients. Whether you are selling cookies, used CDs or whole television networks, **you need clients**.

Lead Generator...

This is a brainstorming exercise about the people that you know that could use your service or product and how often they might need the service.

Keep a list for the next two days of everyone that you come in contact with who could use your service or buy your product.

You'll be surprised how many people you actually speak to every day. Next to their name, make a note as to why you think they would want what you are selling and how to contact them. Start writing below, as you need more room, go to the back of the book. Good luck!

NAME	INFO & WHY?
_____	_____
_____	_____
_____	_____
_____	_____
_____	_____
_____	_____

Frida Kahlo

- Artist, Personality
- Mexico City, Mexico

WHAT SHE DID:

- Continued in the face of strong adversity
- Kept true to her vision

It is said that true art is often borne of pain and this has never been truer than in the case of the great Mexican painter, Frida Kahlo. In 1925, at the age of eighteen, Frida was in a horrible bus accident that left her near death.

After she emerged from a full body cast, Frida was determined to live life on her own terms. She expressed the pain she would always feel through her art. Frida began painting as a way to pass the time while she healed.

At first she was not too good, but she forced herself to keep working on her skills. Before she died in 1954, Frida became world famous for her work and for the power that came from within her. Frida used this power to help her sell her paintings and to turn herself into a celebrity.

Frida lived a life as a true artist, never giving into her own pain nor the views of other people who wished she would live a more traditional lifestyle. Frida remains an inspiration to young artists everywhere and her popularity only continues to grow with the passage of time.

CLOSE THE DEAL

The best salespeople are the ones that are able to turn the most leads into customers or clients. To do this, you must be able to convince the lead (person) that they need your product or service and that your price is too good to refuse. Think about the advertising you see every day. How do they try and turn you into a customer?

Watch your TV...

Watch TV for an hour during the evening. Write down some notes on how the commercials try to get you to buy their products. Think about what you feel works and what doesn't.

Write down an example of a phrase or image that made you want to buy the product.

Next, write an example of a phrase or image that didn't work for you.

_____

_____

_____

_____

EARNING MONEY:

KNOW YOUR PRODUCT...

Take the information you learned from watching the commercials and start working on your own commercial. Write what your selling and why someone should buy it. Keep it short, no more than forty-five words.

If you can't describe what you're selling in less than that, your lead will be asleep before you finish. Try reading it to a friend or family member. Remember, be confident and polite when you're making a sale. Don't worry if what you write is not perfect the first time. You can rework it later.

_____

_____

_____

_____

_____

_____

_____

FOLLOW THROUGH

When a customer or client buys from you a second time it is called **repeat business**. Repeat business is important to all companies. Your time and effort were put into finding those clients and turning them from leads into customers. Make the most of those efforts.

Auction Time...

Look around your room. Are there things that you're not using anymore that you could sell? Make a list of the things you think might be worth something to someone else. Bring the list to your parents and make sure they approve of you selling the items.

Tell them it helps clean the clutter out of your room and helps you start your savings account!

Figure out what amount you want to sell the items for. With the help of your parents, list them online through eBay or have a sale and see what sells.

When your auctions are done, think about what sold and why.

The Soda Caper...

Find a store that sells soda or water in large packs, like 24-packs. Figure out what the cost of each can or bottle is by dividing the total cost by the number in the pack. That becomes the unit cost.

Set the price of each can or bottle just below the price of the same item in a vending machine; this becomes the selling price.

For example if it's 75¢ in a vending machine, you could sell it for 65¢. Sell cans to your friends and schoolmates at a hot baseball game or at the beach. Keep track of how many you sell.

Calculate how much you are making off of each sale by subtracting the unit cost from the selling price. Multiply this amount by the number of cans you expect to sell to see what your profit will be.

$$\frac{\text{PACK COST}}{\text{} } \Big/ \frac{\text{\# OF CANS}}{\text{}} = \frac{\text{UNIT COST}}{\text{}}$$

$$\left(\frac{\text{SELLING PRICE}}{\text{}} - \frac{\text{UNIT COST}}{\text{}} \right) \times \frac{\text{CANS SOLD}}{\text{}} = \frac{\text{YOUR PROFIT}}{\text{}}$$

Out of the Box...

Use your skills. Everyone has skills that are marketable. The trick is identifying them. If you like comic books and you like to draw, start doing your own comic book.

Don't be afraid. Do something that you like and you may find that others like it too. If you like comics but you don't want to learn how to draw or write, then go find someone who does and partner with them. Write below something out of the box that you could do!

_____

_____

_____

Share the News...

Have you already tried starting your own company? Go to **gotmoola.com** and let us know what you did. You'll get to read about others like yourself who are taking control of their future. Share your successes and setbacks, read what others like you have said and maybe you will get some good ideas for your next enterprise!

Pleasant Rowland

- Company: Pleasant Company®
- Middleton, Wisconsin

WHAT SHE DID:
- Recognized an underserved market
- Kept true to her vision

In 1986, Pleasant Rowland felt that the media and toy markets weren't addressing a group that she felt needed attention, seven- to twelve-year-old girls.

Pleasant wanted to create toys that captured the interest and imagination of her target market, and hopefully let kids be kids, just a little longer. At that time Pleasant was forty-five and many industry critics thought that her business, Pleasant Company, was doomed for failure. Many people felt that a line of historical dolls for older girls would never sell. Little did they know!

By combining books and lots of accessories, like mini tea sets and vintage clothing with the dolls, Pleasant turned her company into the second highest selling doll company in America. 2001 sales were a staggering $350 million.

Her line, American Dolls Collection®, combines the things that were important to Pleasant: imagination, history and values. In 1998, Mattel® bought Pleasant Company from Pleasant for $700 million. Pleasant has since retired.

COOL JOBS

COOL JOB #1 – FACT CHECKER

Potential Earnings: $5 to $15 per hour based upon client.

Do you like to read about history and fun stuff? Be a fact checker. Tell your older brothers and sister (and your friends' older siblings too) that you'll help them with their papers for school. When they write papers, they don't always have time to double check all the dates and names. You can do it for them. Now they'll have a great paper and you'll know Abe Lincoln's middle name!

You can also put flyers out in offices. You'll be surprised how often people need research done. In order to do it you will have to be very organized. If you're a messy, sloppy, artistic sort, this probably isn't the thing for you. You can do it from the library or your home computer via the internet. Go to a search engine and type in the subject you are looking for and you're on your way to being a fact checker.

COOL JOB #2 – NEWSLETTER

Potential Earnings: $1 per issue or more because of advertising.

Make your own newsletter! Once a week, or maybe just once a month, you can create your own newsletter! You can make it about something you really care about, like collecting dolls or dancing or a particular Pro Football team or a specific Band. If you care about something this much, there are probably other people who also care a lot. These people will buy your newsletter if it's easily accessible and inexpensive. The other thing to make it about is something that you have a good insight into, for example your neighborhood. You could go from door to door and interview everyone on your street and then put out a newsletter for your neighborhood and see who will pay you for it.

COOL JOB #3 – PARTY TIME

Potential Earnings: From $10 to thousands.

Isn't it great to go to birthday parties? Well, it's not easy to put them on, especially for parents of little kids. If given the option of having a bright young person run the party for them at a reasonable fee, they will take it. Think about how much fun it would be to create parties for a dozen six year olds or ten girls who are in kindergarten. **Make a party-in-a-box!** Write down a bunch of ideas for birthday party themes like the Wild West or the circus. Then find out how much it would cost to buy supplies for the party. Add up the cost of streamers, gift bags, games, and a cake for each theme.

Pass a flyer out to everyone you know with little kids so that they know that they can get a Party taken care of for one cost. They pick the theme, you take it from there. This is a business where your charges can run from $25 up to Thousands! If you get really good at this some person may hire you to put on a huge party for hundreds of people. With planning, work and promotion you'll start making tons of moola!

COOL JOB #4 – DOODLE WEAR

Potential Earnings: Make a shirt for $7 and sell it for $15.

Do you like to draw? Have you ever drawn a cartoon when you should have been doing your homework? Well, now you can turn those drawings into money. Let the clubs and sports teams at your school know that you can design shirts for them. Show them a few of your best drawings so they can see your talent. You can make cool pictures for the track team and the drama club and they can put those drawings on their T-shirts. Your art will be all over school, and your friends will have cool one-of-a-kind shirts!

COOL JOB #5 - PET CARE

Potential Earnings: $10 to $25 per week or $3 to $5 per day

Do you like animals? Imagine getting paid to spend time with them! Lots of people have to leave their pets with strangers when they leave town. From fish or iguanas that have to be fed, to dogs that need to be walked, people have animals that they need cared for when they leave town. Kennels are very expensive and inconvenient. Plus, their pets would rather stay in their house where they can run in their own yard or park. Now, you can help. Be a pet-sitter! You can visit your neighbors' houses a couple of times a day, maybe before and after school, and feed and walk your neighbors' pets.

You get to spend time with animals and your neighbors will know that their pets are in good hands. You can also be a plant-sitter. No, you won't have to walk a fern around the block, you can just water your neighbors' plants so when they get back from vacation all their plants will be green and healthy. With one flyer you can let everyone in your neighborhood know.

COOL JOB #6 - WEB CRITIC

Potential Earnings: $25 per teen critique

Do you love making web sites? Do you go to web sites aimed at young people like you that are completely missing the boat? Well, here is an opportunity. Email the owners of each site you visit that has a poor interface. You can fix all that. If you don't do the coding yourself you could contact the webmasters for these sites and tell them you'll be their teen-for-hire. You can let the webmasters know what's wrong and what's right from a teen point-of-view. They'll appreciate your feedback and you'll be a big part of making a better web site. Charge them $25 for your analysis.

EARNING MONEY:

COOL JOB #7 – GOOD OLD FASHIONED WORK

Potential Earnings: Charge $5 to $10 for every hour of your time.
Spend your weekends outside! All you need is a rake in the fall, a shovel in the winter, and a lawnmower in the summer. Put fliers in your neighbors' mailboxes to let them know that you can help them keep their lawns looking good and their sidewalks clear of snow. If you do a good job for one person, they'll tell their friends and soon, you'll be getting paid to spend your weekends in the sun!

COOL JOB #8 – PET FINDER

Potential Earnings: Varies based on how many posters you put up.
You can help find lost pets. When a pet runs away the owners can only put up a few posters by themselves, but with your help, they can put up posters all over town. Start a poster distribution business! Make copies and put them up in stores and around the neighborhood. All you need is a bike and a lot of energy. Put flyers up on bulletin boards in Pet Stores and Grocery Stores letting people know that you can help them get their lost pet back.

COOL JOB #9 – TECHY FOR HIRE

Potential Earnings: $10 to $20 for every hour of your time.
Were you the one to hook up your parents' new DVD player? Did you have to teach your mom how to use e-mail? Not everybody has a kid as smart as you in their own house to help them. You can change all that. Be a technology tutor! Help your neighbors and friends learn to get the most form their new computers and TVs. You may be the person that they're looking for.

COOL JOB #10 - WORK WITH YOUR PARENTS

Potential Earnings: Charge $5 to $10 for every hour of your time.
If either of your parents own a business, they might be able to use your help. Even if they work for another company, they may be able to hook you up with a part-time job there. If you're good at organization, your parents may need help preparing their files for taxes during the year.

COOL JOB #11 - HELP AT A CAMP

Potential Earnings: $200 to $1000 depending on the camp
Contact the groups that run camps in your area. You could work with kids, tend the grounds, prepare food, or do any of a number of things. Summer is the busiest time for camps but there are often camps that run year-round. Many communities have after school programs for kids that may need counselors to help. Ask at your school or check online.

COOL JOB #12 - WORK AT A RETAIL STORE

Potential Earnings: $7 to $10 per hour depending on the store.
One big benefit to working at a store that you often shop at is the discount that you may receive for things you buy at the store (which can be substantial) and commissions on items you sell. Retail stores must comply with labor laws which may not allow them to hire you if you are under fifteen years old.

COOL JOB #13 - AID THE ELDERLY

Potential Earnings: Charge $5 to $10 for every hour of your time.
Some older people have difficulty getting around. They may welcome your services delivering groceries, running errands, or doing odd jobs around their home. Ask your parents and neighbors you know.

COOL JOB #14 - RECYCLER

Potential Earnings: Varies based on how much you recycle

Make money helping the environment! Do you recycle? Do your neighbors? If you live in a neighborhood with no recycling truck, let your neighbors know that you will help them recycle. A lot of people want to help the earth, but don't have time to drive all the way to a recycling center. You can help. Choose a day every week to visit your neighbors and pick up all their bottles and cans. Then you can take them to the recycling center. Most centers will pay about 5¢ per can, depending on what state you live in. You'll be making some money and saving the planet too! But remember, once you tell people that you will take all their recyclables you have to go collect them, and that's not necessarily a whole lot of fun. So this one is suggested for young people that love nature and care about the environment. It's a good way to blend a belief with a business. Plus, the end result is that you're helping the planet and increasing your assets with periodic cash payments.

More Cool Jobs...

Looking for more cool job ideas? Do you have an idea that you'd like to share? Go to **gotmoola.com** and check out the latest list of cool job ideas from our experts and from other kids just like you. Work should be fun and this is the place to start!

WRITE YOUR OWN BUSINESS IDEAS...

_____

_____

_____

_____

_____

_____

_____

_____

_____

_____

_____

_____

_____

_____

_____

_____

_____

EARNING MONEY:

WRITE YOUR OWN BUSINESS IDEAS...

_____

_____

_____

_____

_____

_____

_____

_____

_____

_____

_____

_____

_____

_____

INVENTION

Inventing a product to sell is an excellent way of beginning a business. People of all ages invented the items you use every day! All it takes is **recognizing a problem**, having **a little creativity**, and the **willingness to experiment**. In fact, you have probably invented things already and didn't even know it. Who knows, maybe years from now people will be reading about you as they learn about making more than their parents.

BETTER SCHOOLS

Create a list of items that would make your life easier at school. Don't worry if the ideas seem too crazy. Remember, brainstorming is an important part of any creative process.

_____

_____

_____

_____

_____

_____

Madame CJ Walker

- Company: Madame Walker's
  Wonderful Hair Grower
- Denver, Colorado

WHAT SHE DID:

- Recognized a need in the market
- Persisted against setbacks

Madame CJ Walker's real name was Sarah and she was born right after the end of slavery in Lousiana. She was orphaned when she was seven years old and the only way to survive was to go work in the cotton fields. When she was sixteen she went to St. Louis where her brothers worked as barbers. Sarah had married very young only to have her husband die, yet she was able to raise and educate her daughter working as a laundry woman. When she was in her twenties, Sarah's hair started to fall out. She found some hair products that helped her. Sarah thought that other women would want them too, so she started work as a sales woman for the products she liked.

In 1905, she moved to Denver, got married, and started selling 'Madame Walker's Wonderful Hair Grower'. She began selling her hair formula door to door. Her sales grew and she added more products and more employees. Before she died, her company had over 3,000 employees, making her the first known African-American woman to become a self-made millionaire. When asked her secret of success, she said… "if I have accomplished anything in life it is because I have been willing to work hard. I am a woman who came from the cotton fields, was promoted to the washtub to the cook kitchen. And from there I promoted myself into the business of manufacturing hair goods and preparations. I have built my own factory on my own ground."

Brandon & Spencer Whale

- Invention: Pacemate
- Biz Whiz @ Ages: 8 and 6

WHAT THEY DID:

- Identified a need
- Combined innovation and giving

If you ever thought that you were too young to do something important; or wondered what it feels like to do something simply out of kindness, then you need to meet Brandon and Spencer Whale.

When he was six years old, Spencer Whale (yes, you read it right, SIX years old! Not sixteen or sixty—six!) Anyway, Spencer was visiting a hospital and noticed that parents had to push IV poles behind kids riding on wheeled toys.

Spencer wondered, "what if the IV poles were on the toys?" He drew a plan (Spencer likes to draw), then made a sample that kids loved. People donated materials, and seven years later he's still making them. Spencer doesn't take money for this. He does it because his family believes in helping others. His roller coaster designs are another matter. He'll charge for those.

Spencer is the youngest person in the National Gallery for America's Young Inventors. Incredibly, he broke the record of his brother, a future doctor, who donated his own amazing invention, too! Now, Spencer and Brandon support the work being done at an incredible place called the Winthrop University Hospital's Cancer Center for Kids, and you can help them at ***www.gotmoola.com***

Learn from the Masters...

Make it a fun hobby to read the biographies of great inventors. Write down the names of three products that you find interesting.

Now read a biography about one of the inventors every six weeks. You can do it. You will discover that some of their creativity will rub off on you.

_____

_____

_____

The Art of You...

If you enjoy arts and crafts, try making jewelry, cards, or other items and sell them -- perhaps on eBay™, or from a stand in a fair, wherever you'll have access to customers. Some painters and photographers are making money selling their work online, too.

Make a few pieces and see if any of them sell. Don't be discouraged if things don't sell at first. Remember, Henry Ford went bankrupt twice before he succeeded with Ford Motor Company™.

GIFTS / AWARDS

While you work towards your new methods of earning money, don't forget the things that have worked in the past. If you're like most of us, the first money you got was a gift, an award or a prize. Maybe it was $5 on your birthday from your grandmother. Maybe it was a contest you entered at school that you won. Whatever it was, don't forget these tried and true ways to earn money. Often, they take very little extra effort on your part and can be a valuable part of your earning arsenal.

Whenever you do get a present from someone, remember to send them a thank-you note and make sure you let them know that their gift is now hard at work in your college fund. The more positive feedback you give to people who help you, the more they will want to help you. **It's human nature. Use it to your advantage**.

> It's okay to try different methods of earning money until you find one that works for you. **The important thing is to just start.**

SCHOLARSHIPS

Millions of dollars are made available each year to students applying for scholarships. Some of them are specific to individual schools or colleges; others are general and can be applied to books, food or whatever will make your studying easier. Scholarships can be awarded

for grades, sports, writing, contests, or even just being you. A common misconception is that only people with good grades or who are good at sports get scholarships. Take the time to find out what is available. We've got a whole list of places waiting for you at *gotmoola.com*.

Thank you so much...

GIFTS – write to all of your relatives, thanking them for their generous birthday presents from last year. This will make them feel good and will keep your birthday in their minds for this year.

Send handwritten notes. Get the addresses from your parents and ask for stamps. If you need to buy some you can get them at the post office.

Grant Your Wish...

AWARDS – Talk to your school counselor and see if there are scholarships or awards that you can apply for. Thousands of awards are offered each year to students just like you. There are also GRANTS that are available sometimes for very unique things.

Ooooh, Contests...

PRIZES – Check the newspaper and web for information on contests and prizes in a subject that you really like. Make sure to check with your parents and be sure to find contests that don't cost you money!

IDEA BANK...

Whenever you get an idea for a job or business or invention, write it down. Once it's written down you can go back and put a plan of action in place for the ideas you like the best. Your ideas are part of your assets. The ability to have these ideas is one of your resources.

Don't worry if you fill up this page, you're supposed to. There are plenty more pages in the back of the book for you to keep writing.

_____

_____

_____

_____

_____

_____

_____

_____

BIZ WHIZ

John Bogle

- Company: Vanguard Group™
- Valley Forge, Pennsylvania

WHAT HE DID:

- Identified a new market
- Provided a system that worked for customers

Can a poor student with some wacky ideas change the world? Absolutely. In John Bogle's case, he did just that.

While at Princeton where he studied economics, Bogle worked hard, but as he puts it, "just didn't get it." Not getting it led Bogle to look at the world of money a little differently than his peers. Instead of studying what had been done before, Bogle wrote his thesis on the business of mutual funds and in doing so, came up with idea for the first index fund.

Index funds allow people to invest in a community of stocks rather than in individual stocks picked by a broker or money manager. Bogle determined that over ten years, only a relative handful of investors were going to beat the market average, so he thought, "why not invest in the market itself?" His first index fund, the Vanguard 500™, wasn't very popular. In fact, it was so unpopular that he didn't have the money to invest in all 500 stocks at first. Today that index fund is the largest mutual fund in the world with over $115 billion in assets. Bogle's company, the Vanguard Group, has become the country's second largest fund company. Not bad for someone whose scholarship was almost revoked for bad grades. (Note: his grades later improved and he graduated magna cum laude.)

Kenya Jordana James

- Company: Blackgirl™ Magazine
- Biz Whiz @ Age: 11

WHAT SHE DID:

- Recognized an underserved market
- Kept true to her vision

When she was in the third grade, Kenya Jordana James noticed that there weren't many positive messages for African-American kids. When she was even, she was so frustrated by the magazines for kids; she decided to create a magazine for girls like her to read. She started *Blackgirl™ Magazine* so that kids like her could see that there are a lot of great role models in the world.

She made $1,200 selling cakes to her neighbors to help her fund her first issue. She also found sponsors and advertisers and created a business plan. Now, *Blackgirl Magazine* is twenty pages long and includes interviews with people like Serena and Venus Williams and Outkast. Kenya has been on *The Oprah Winfrey Show*™ and has been interviewed on the radio. It has helped her get interviews with big stars like Lauren Hill. Her magazine isn't just about celebrities, though. Her magazine is also about African-American culture and history. A lot of adults who make magazines didn't think that kids wanted to know about anything more than music and fashion. Kenya knew they were wrong. Now, *Blackgirl Magazine* has 4,000 subscribers and is sold in several states. Even though starting her own magazine was hard, Kenya knew she could do it. "You're never too young to do something that's worth doing."

73

Debbie Fields

- Company: Mrs. Fields®
- Palo Alto, California

WHAT SHE DID:

- Recognized a new market
  angle for growth
- Kept true to her vision

Debbie Fields loves cookies (who doesn't?!), but she never expected that her cookies would make her a millionaire!

Ever since she was young, Debbie baked cookies. She brought her chocolate chip cookies to school and gave them to her friends. They all called her the "cookie kid." Debbie always knew she had a great recipe and she dreamed of opening up a store. But no one else thought she could. No candy, no cakes, just cookies.

Debbie had no experience running a store, she hadn't been to college and she was only twenty years old, but she had faith in herself. So Debbie started baking and let the great taste of her cookies bring the customers. When she started her business, a lot of people told her she would fail, but Debbie didn't listen. That was twenty years ago. Now, you can get Mrs. Fields® cookies almost anywhere you go!

Debbie had to listen to a lot of people tell her "no" on her way to success. A lot of people didn't believe in her, but Debbie knew that the most important thing was to believe in herself. "The important thing is not being afraid to take a chance. Remember, the greatest failure is to not try. Once you find something you love to do, be the best at doing it."

CHAPTER 3

SPENDING MONEY

Spending money is fun!!! You are in charge. Everyone wants your money, including you. Whether you are spending money to buy T-shirts that you are going to print and sell, buying a week at a camp for young musicians or buying some very cool clothes, you should **think before you spend.**

Spending money can give you great satisfaction. Avoid throwing away money on stuff you're only going to care about for an hour. That way you get the most bang for your buck... and you become more powerfully motivated to earn your money.

SPENDING MONEY:

The trick to spending your money is doing it in such a way that you get to have fun with it WHILE you increase the value of your portfolio. That way as time goes on, you'll be able to continue having fun with your money without worrying about going broke along the way. Aha! We are back to **FINANCIAL FREEDOM!** Remember, that's how you win! Now, let's look at some of the secrets you can use to spend your money wisely.

1. THINK BEFORE YOU BUY

The first secret is the most obvious. **Think before you buy something**. Purchasing without thinking is so common that stores have even given it its own name: **impulse shopping**. Limit your impulsive buys to things equal to or less in price than a single scoop of ice cream.

2. TAKE A BREATH

Next time you're out and you see that new game or shirt or CD that you just "have to have," think about whether you need to buy it right now. **Can it wait a day?** Often times the same item that seemed so cool the first time you saw it doesn't seem that great the next time or is available for a lot less. If you're not sure, try walking around the store for a while, carrying the item with you. Look around at all the other items. Think about how long it took you to earn the money you're about to spend and how long it will take to replace that money. You'd be surprised how often you'll end up putting the item back.

DISCIPLINE! When you exercise something, it grows stronger. Excercising your discipline puts you in charge of your money and your future. Don't let money ever be the boss of you. When you tell it to sit, it sits. Tell it to go get a bike, it goes and gets a bike.

3. COMPARE BUT BE REAL

Comparing prices is an easy way to save. Finding stores that have the best prices can save you a lot of money on the things you like to buy. This is called **comparison shopping**. Finding a store that sells the soda you like for 50¢ instead of 75¢ is great, but don't spend all day looking for it. For smaller priced items, say under $20, the savings may not justify the effort. Remember, your time is valuable too. Finding stores that you know have good prices on things that you purchase the most is good enough.

COMPARISON EXAMPLE FROM CHECKING ONLINE
A NEW PDA   RETAIL PRICE: $299 + 5% tax (average) = $314

Online Store	S&H	Price	Total	Difference
Web Store 1	$14	$266	$280	-$34
Web Store 2	$10	$279	$289	-$25
Web Store 3	free	$299	$299	-$15
Web Store 4	$6	$295	$301	-$13
Web Store 5	$10	$334	$344	+$30
Web Store 6	$9	$388	$397	+$83

The exception to this is with larger, one-time purchases. This is where Comparison Shopping can really save the day. Luckily, Comparison Shopping has been made much easier thanks to the Internet.

While you don't have to make the purchase online, you can check the prices of many different kinds of items online so that you are educated about how much something should cost. Above is an example of a good product price comparison. Which place is the best buy? Online or Retail?

4. QUALITY IS KEY

Don't be afraid to spend a little bit more for something that is of recognized quality. **Quality has a lot of value**. Doing research on an item before you buy it can help you make the best decision. For example, before you buy a bike, talk to your friends who do a lot of biking about what they like and don't like about their bikes. There's no reason to repeat their mistakes. Next, go online and look up Web sites that compare bikes and review them. The company that makes the bike will always say it's the best, so try to find a source like a bike magazine Web site that doesn't make money by selling you bikes. Once you know more about what makes a good bike, you'll be able to buy your bike with confidence. Plus, it's fun learning about something you're going to own. It makes it more special and meaningful.

5. BRANDS AND BARGAINS

At your age, you are part of the biggest target audience of ad campaigns pushing the importance of "brands." Manufacturers spend millions of dollars trying to make you believe that their product makes you jump higher, look better, run faster, get more dates, or be more accepted just because of the logo on their product. Part of being a smart consumer is educating yourself on the difference between hype and reality. Reading reviews and, if possible, talking with experts can help you sort out the truth behind the advertising. Remember, ads and commercials are designed to make you spend your money on their products. Think about why you are buying one brand over another before you part with your money.

6. REBATES, SALES AND COUPONS, OH MY!

We've all seen the "$5 Off Mail-In Offer" coupon attached to an item in the store. Sometimes we even buy the product because of the coupon, thinking to ourselves what a great deal we're getting. Then, when we get home, we end up throwing out the coupon with the packaging because it seems like too big of a hassle. These coupons are actually advertisements designed to entice you to buy the product. Studies show that 95 percent of the people that bought the product didn't take the time to mail in the rebate. The companies that print them count on this laziness. Before you buy a product because of a cash-back offer, think about whether you will actually send in the rebate. If not, you may be paying more than you should.

Likewise, retailers will often send you coupons in the mail offering special discounts or notices about limited-time sales events. Retailers rely on people visiting their stores. They are betting that these offers will encourage you to go to their store over other stores, even if you don't need their products. They know that once you're there, you will probably buy more than the offer requires and they will be able to take more of your money. Just because a store offers a coupon or is having a sale doesn't mean that you should buy the product.

Not all coupons are bad. In fact, coupons can be an excellent way to save money. Using coupons for the things you normally buy allows you to beat the companies at their own game. Make coupons work for you, not the other way around.

Clippity-clip...

Take notes on what items your family buys on a regular basis. Then, go through the coupons that come with the newspaper. See how many of the items on your list have coupons. It may not be many. Place the ones that match in an envelope marked "COUPONS." The next time you go to the store, bring the envelope and see how much you save.

Coupons for Cash...

Do a food inventory for the people in your neighborhood. Provide them with coupons on a weekly basis for the things they use. Charge three dollars a week, and save them five dollars, so you both win. If you get ten people that's thirty bucks a week!

FUTURE PLANNING (GOALS)

You've probably heard your parents talk about budgeting. All that means is that you should keep track of how much you make, spend, save, and then choose wisely where your money goes. Being on a budget isn't a bad thing, it just means that you have plans for your money (like making more of it!) and don't want to spend it on silly things.

Keeping a budget gives you the power to meet your goals and not wonder why your money keeps disappearing. If you want to make more than your parents, **it's a good idea to begin setting goals.** Remember when we talked about big goals like owning your own music studio, amusement park or pro-sports team? Those goals take time to happen, but there are things that you can start planning for immediately. If there's a bike that you'd like to get, you'll need to find out how much it costs and how long it will take you to save up the money. If you're thinking about starting your own business, you'll need to make a plan for what materials you'll need, how much they cost, and how long it will take you to get the money.

Another way of thinking of purchases is to buy items that will satisfy your desire for cool stuff AND help you to build your wealth (this is a bit of a brain twister). Let's say that you are going to use a bike to start delivering flyers for a restaurant in your neighborhood, once a week, for $20. Your capacity to earn money will be higher once you have the bike. Your bike is part of your assets. Now, you're starting to think like an entrepreneur!

I SPENT HOW MUCH?!

Keep track of what you spend over the course of a day. Throughout the day, write in the amount you spent and what you spent it on. At the end of the day, add up the total. You may be surprised how much you have spent. Use this information to help you spend less during the next day.

DESCRIPTION	COST $
_____	_____
_____	_____
_____	_____
_____	_____
_____	_____
TOTAL:	_____

BIG BAD DEBT

When you're in debt, it means that you owe more money than you have. That money could be owed to a credit card company, a bank, a school or even a friend or family member. The best way to deal with debt is to avoid getting into it in the first place. This means that, starting today, you should try to spend less money than you earn. Sounds easy, right? It can be. The problem most people get into is that they allow themselves just a little bit of debt so that they can buy something they think they really want, like a new game. However, they're more likely to spend their money on a second game before they're done paying for the first game. Next thing you know, the debt has grown to the size of a giant beast, larger than anything in any game, and fighting it just got a lot harder.

IS DEBT ALWAYS BAD?

There will be things in your life that you'll want that you won't be able to afford without credit, like a car or a house. When starting your own business, most people need to borrow money to get things going. Most institutions need proof that you can responsibly handle having debt. They look at a score that you've been assigned called your **credit rating**. Just like colleges use your grades to tell what classes you took and how you did in them, banks and other lenders read your credit history to tell how you have paid back companies that have lent you money in the past. If your credit rating isn't high enough, they can refuse to lend you the money. The more responsibly you handle your finances now, the more responsibly you'll handle credit and the better rates you'll get for that.

SO WHAT DO I DO?

While starting a credit history is a good idea, you should talk to your parents about it before you do anything. They probably have strong feelings about credit cards and may be able to offer some advice. If they are willing to get you a starter credit card, you should charge only small items and pay off the entire balance on the card each month. This way you avoid large interest payments, while starting to build a positive credit history.

To learn more about credit cards, keep reading, or go to *gotmoola.com* and try out the credit card tools!

IT JUST COSTS TOO MUCH...

Write down items that you would like to buy someday that you know cost too much for you to afford right now. Go to the web site and find out how much you would pay for each of these items if you bought them on a credit card and only paid the minimum due.

_____   _____

_____   _____

_____   _____

WAYS TO PAY

CASH

It isn't all about the Benjamins. The Jacksons, the Lincolns and the Washingtons are good too. Accepted almost everywhere you can buy something, cash is the preferred method of payment at most stores. Why? Because most other ways to pay are like IOU's written by you to the store. With cash, the store knows that the item has been paid for. Right now, cash is the best way for you to pay for things too. Checks and credit cards can make it easy to pretend you have more money than you do.

The problem with cash is that it can be bulky if you try to carry around a lot of it. It can also be unsafe. If you drop your money, anyone can pick it up and spend it. For these reasons, banks created a number of ways that are more convenient for you to pay for what you want. Most of them require you to be 18 or have your parents co-sign with you before they'll give you access. Let's look through a couple of the options so you can start planning for the future.

CHECKS

Checks are a more convenient way of paying than cash. When you want to pay for an item, you write a check for the cost of the item and sign it over to the store. The store then sends that check to their own bank to be deposited, or placed into their account. When the store's bank receives the check, they send a message to your bank requesting the money. If you have enough in your bank account, the money is withdrawn from your account and transferred to the store's bank where it is placed in the store's account.

Unlike cash, however, you CAN spend more than you have with checks. When you do, the bank will refuse payment on the check to the store and you will probably end up paying fines (at least $25!). This is called an **overdraft**. The check is said to have "bounced." For this reason it is crucial that you keep your checking account balanced. That means that you know how much money is in your account. It's actually quite easy. To begin, write the amount of money you have in the bank account on your checkbook's balance sheet.

Then, as you make purchases with the checkbook, write down the amounts, a brief description and the date. After each purchase, subtract the amount you spent from the remaining amount you have in the account. The remaining amount is called your balance. *Voilà!* You've just balanced your checkbook! You can check how well you're doing by comparing your balanced amount to the amount online if your bank offers online accounts.

WHAT'S ON A CHECK?

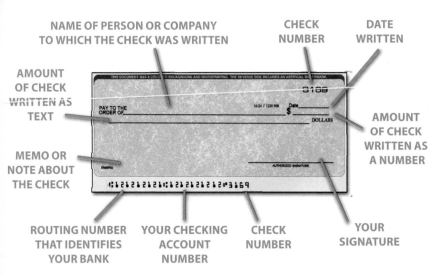

SPENDING MONEY:

ATM / CASH CARD

Cash cards can be used to take money out of your accounts when at a cash machine or Automatic Teller Machine (ATM). The card is the same size as a credit card and comes with a security PIN (Personal Identification Number), a password that you use to prove that it is you that is using the card. Upon entering the code at the cash machine, you have the ability to remove cash from your bank account up to the amount that the bank has set as your limit (normally $300/day).

Some businesses allow you to use the card to pay for goods like groceries or gas. Your PIN is needed every time you use the card. The downside to buying things this way is that the banks often charge you each time you use the card away from the bank. It can cost you three or four dollars if you take money out from the wrong machine. To increase the usefulness of cash cards, most banks have partnered with either VISA or MasterCard to allow their cash cards to be used wherever credit cards are accepted. These enhanced cards are called check cards or debit cards.

CHECK / DEBIT CARD

One more way to pay is an extended version of a cash card called a check card. Check cards won't let you spend much more than what you have in your account. That's because, unlike a credit card, a check card withdraws the amount of your purchase from your bank account. Normally your check card is linked to your checking account, but you can have it linked to other accounts depending on your needs. Just like your checkbook, however, a check card can cause overdrafts. The bank tries to help you avoid this by limiting the amounts that you can charge on the check card in a single day. This is similar to the withdraw limit set on your ATM card. If you try to make a purchase larger than this amount, the card may be rejected.

Check cards have three big advantages:

1 - It's easier to limit your spending because of daily spending limits and its connection to your bank account.

2 - You can use this Check Card at most stores around the country to make your purchases. Check cards are normally accepted anywhere that credit cards are accepted.

3 - Because the purchases are tied to your bank account, you will have access to a monthly record of the card's use. It's an excellent way to keep a budget, especially if your bank offers online banking.

Check cards can be very useful. However, it is still very important for you to keep track of your account balance. For more information about getting a check card and viewing your bank account online go to the web site *gotmoola.com*

CREDIT CARDS

Credit cards have become increasingly popular over the last twenty years. Most people have at least one credit card. When you make a purchase on a credit card, you are basically borrowing money from the company that issued you the card. That's the easy part. Credit cards become tricky when it comes time to pay back what you borrowed. Many people who use credit cards discover that each month when their credit cards become due, they don't have enough money to pay back the amount borrowed.

This is exactly what credit card companies count on. They make their money by charging you **interest**, or a percentage, on the amount that you borrowed. The longer it takes you to pay back the money, the more money they make. In fact, the interest on that amount can add up to MORE than amount you borrowed if you're not careful! That's why so many people have bad debt.

To protect young people from misusing their credit cards, the government does not allow people under eighteen to sign up for a credit card without their parents signing up as well. If your parents are willing, you may sign up for your first credit card. To help make sure people don't go crazy with how much they charge, credit card companies place a limit on how much you can spend. This limit, along with how much interest you will pay them, is set primarily based on your credit history.

If you are just starting out, your credit history may keep you from getting a high limit. Common limits range from $300 to $1,000 for first time card holders. If you try to spend more than your limit, you may get fined by the credit company and run the risk of being embarrassed at the store or restaurant when your card is refused. The best way of avoiding this is to always **stay aware of how much you have charged** and how soon you can pay it back.

Some credit card companies offer secure credit cards for people with bad or weak credit histories. A secure card works a little like a debit card. When you sign up, the bank sets the limit on the card by an amount that you must keep in your bank account. For example, if a bank requires that you have $300 in an account before getting a secure card, then your limit of spending on that card would be $300.

We have more information about credit cards online, but for now, here are some things you should keep in mind about these difficult little pieces of plastic.

1 – Talk to your parents about credit cards before ever signing up for one, especially if you're under eighteen.

2 – Avoid offers from small companies or stores to sign up for their credit card. These cards will often charge you very high percentage rates and can only be used at that specific store. What a pain!

3 – Keep track of what you purchase. When your bill arrives, be sure to pay it in full right away. This way, you can keep your interest payment low and your credit history in good standing. Don't view your credit card limit as a goal. The goal should be staying as far away from that limit as possible.

	PROs	CONs
CASH	Widely accepted No cost to use	Very insecure Can be bulky
CHECK	Widely accepted Easy to carry	Possible to overspend Requires balancing
CASH CARD	Easiest to carry Relatively secure	Limited purchasing Not widely accepted
CHECK CARD	Easiest to carry Relatively secure	Possible to overspend Limited purchasing
CREDIT CARD	Easiest to carry Largest purchasing	Easy to acquire debt Highest cost

REMEMBER:

Never Shop on Impulse!

Meet your ongoing savings goals.

Remember how hard you worked.

Spend your money wisely.

By combining what you learned in this chapter (good budgeting, solid account balancing and smart shopping) you'll find it easier than ever to afford the things you want. Credit card companies, loan offices and banks will see that you're responsible and help you along the way. You'll need them to be on your side when you want to buy the really cool things like a car, a house, or when you're starting your first business!

Now that you're an expert on spending the money that you've earned, let's talk about the best ways of keeping that money. Did you know that the money you save can actually earn you MORE money? Let's find out how...

Even if you're on the right track,
you'll get run over if you just sit there.
— Will Rogers

BANK ON IT...
Can you solve the mystery?

A Bank President catches two employees in his vault. They both say they caught the other one trying to steal a bag of coins. One of the two states loudly that he has no interest in old Spanish coins and that if he hadn't come along the other employee would be long gone. In fact, he had seen her drop something in her purse. Before the woman can move, her accuser reaches over, flicks open the clasp, reaches into her purse and pulls out a coin, which he reveals with a flourish. The Bank President smiles and tells security to have the man arrested and to give the woman a reward for her honesty and bravery.

How did he know the man was the robber?

Answer – First, how did he know that the bag held Spanish coins? Secondly, he spoke, loudly as if on a stage and then opened her purse and displayed the coin with a flourish. The Banker guessed that the man was an amateur magician quite capable of hiding a coin in his palm.

Florence Nightingale

- Revolutionary Nurse
- London, England

WHAT SHE DID:
- Helped those less fortunate
- Stayed true to her vision

Florence Nightingale's parents were wealthy and wanted to give her everything she asked for. But Florence didn't want to take, she wanted to give. She had a natural instinct to take care of people. She decided the best way to do it was to become a nurse. However, it wasn't considered fitting for wealthy women to work in a little dirty office with sick people. Florence didn't listen. After going to college in Germany, she decided to help the wounded soldiers in the Crimean War. This was in 1854.

When Florence got to the army hospital, she knew she had to do something to help the men get better treatment. Most people didn't yet understand the dangerous infections that occur in dirty conditions, but Florence did. Florence worked with the army and a newspaper in London to raise money and to organize better hospitals for the wounded soldiers. She did all of this in less than one year! Florence became very famous and used her fame to help soldiers get better and better care. She wrote books and met with royalty and presidents throughout the world. Florence started her own school of nursing in London and by the time of her death, nursing was one of the most honored professions anyone could ever choose. Florence was driven to help other people. She helped save the lives of countless people and had an incredible life to boot.

CHAPTER 4

SAVING MONEY

It may seem odd, but saving money is one of the best ways to increase the money you have! That's right, this is common sense. We're not talking about brain surgery here. The easiest way of saving money is to not spend it. Just hold onto it and put it in smart places. With that said, let's look at a couple of things you can do with your money that will make it more fun to save.

The money you save can actually earn you more money. At first, it may not seem like much, but if you follow a regular savings plan you'll see your money grow faster and faster, all by itself. The day you hit Financial Freedom is the day that you can live the way you want to live, and pay for everything, out of the money you get each year as **interest** or **dividends** on your savings.

For example, a person with $2 million dollars in their portfolio may safely earn 6 percent interest every year on that money. This equals $120,000 per year in interest. If they can live their ideal lifestyle for $100,000 per year, they have reached financial freedom. They get to do whatever they want, and the value of their portfolio keeps going up.

PIGGY BANKS AND BURIED TREASURE

Wealthy people have understood the importance of saving money for as long as money has existed. Before there were banks, people would keep their money in locked rooms or chests. Tales of buried treasure originated because pirates would hide their money, trying to keep it safe from other pirates who might steal it. Of course, if they lost their treasure map or forgot where they put it, they'd be in a bit of trouble.

A locked box or even a piggy bank is a good place to start saving money. If you want, you can make a custom bank out of materials around your house. This way, when you find that you have extra money, just put it in your customized piggy bank and pretend it's not there.

At the end of each month, take the money you've saved and deposit it into your bank account.

If you don't have a bank account yet—don't worry. We are about to look at how you can set one up!

Bank in a Bottle...

Find an empty or near-empty 2-liter clear plastic soda bottle (a juice or water bottle will work). Rinse out the bottle. When the bottle is dry, cut off the top of the bottle so that a hole, smaller than your hand at the top.

If you like, you can decorate the bottle with some paper, markers and glue. Place the bottle in your room near the door or your bed. Every day, when you come home, empty the change from your pockets and put it in to the bottle.

When the bottle fills, take it to the bank to deposit the money into an account (see the next section), and start again.

BANK ACCOUNTS

The first banks, as we know them, came into existence in the fifteenth century in Amsterdam, Holland. However, for the average person, banking did not become commonplace until the twentieth century.

Initially, banks offered only a secure place to keep or trade your money so that you didn't have to carry it with you. This may seem simple, but it was a big deal in olden days.

Luckily, we have many options available to us today. Banks have become companies that provide people with many ways of saving and investing money. Most parents have at least one account at their bank. Talking to them about their experiences with their bank can give you a good idea if it's where you want to open your account.

Remember, the bank wants **YOU** as a customer. Be sure that the bank offers the services you want, like online banking, low fees, and friendly help. If they don't, there are many other banks that will. Don't be afraid to look around. You can also get accounts online with banks in far away places.

 A bank is like any other company. It earns money by having you as a customer. Many banks will make claims that they are the best.

Go to the *gotmoola.com* site to learn more about the options that you should look for when choosing a bank. Let's talk about the basic accounts you need to consider for your portfolio right now and in the near future.

SAVINGS ACCOUNTS

Besides being a safe place to keep your money, savings accounts are interest earning, meaning that the bank pays you to keep your money in the account. This is a great way to start having your money make more money for you!

Some banks require a **minimum balance**, an amount of money required to open the account. Find out what that amount is and begin saving for it. When you've saved enough, go to your local bank and talk to them about opening an account. If you're under eighteen, you'll want to bring your parents along with you.

CHECKING ACCOUNTS

A checking account is similar to a savings account. The biggest difference is that a checking account is designed to have money taken out of it. Each check is a promise that you write to someone you want to buy something from that says that they will be paid the amount on the check by your bank. Checks are very useful, as most companies do not accept cash when paying bills by mail. If you start your own company, you'll need to start a checking account in order to pay your company's bills. Banks offer different options like personalized checks or duplicate checks for your records. Be smart about which options you choose. Remember you're there to save money, not to spend it.

To review the different options to watch for when opening a checking account, visit the *gotmoola.com* site. There you can also find more information about writing, transferring or depositing checks.

SAVING MONEY:

DEPOSITS

Making a deposit means that you are putting money that you have earned or saved into your bank account. There are many ways of doing this. Most banks require that you fill-out a deposit slip when you arrive at the bank or ATM. This slip tells the bank which of your accounts you want the money put into.

You can also make a form of deposit, called a transfer of funds, from one account to another. This may allow you to take advantage of more lucrative opportunities within your portfolio. Some banks offer deposit books that are stamped when you make a deposit and will help you keep track of your account transactions. Otherwise the bank will provide written and/or online updates for your accounts.

WITHDRAWALS

Making a withdrawal means that you are taking money out of your bank account. There are many ways of doing this, such as using your **checkbook**, your **debit card**, or your **check card** (see the spending chapter). Banks also allow you to remove funds by filling out a withdrawal slip and giving it to a teller at the bank. Remember that you worked very hard for the money in your accounts, so think before you withdraw funds.

FDIC – BACKING YOUR BANK

The Federal Deposit Insurance Corporation protects the money that you deposit in your bank account up to $100,000. This means that even if the bank goes bankrupt, your money is still safe. The FDIC also sponsors other programs that help consumers and communities.

BONDS/CDS

A bond is basically a loan. The big difference between this loan and others that have been discussed in this book is that **YOU** are loaning the money. The group you loan the money to gives you the bond as a promise to repay the amount you lent them at a specific date in the future, plus interest.

The Bond Market vs. The Stock Market

TOTAL OUTSTANDING VALUE - 2002

STOCKS: $8.9 trillion

BONDS: $11.1 trillion

Bonds are sold by bond dealers who work at banks and security firms. They buy bonds from the government and corporations and sell them to you. Today's U.S. bond market is the largest securities market in the world, larger even than the U.S. stock market.

The bond market is considered **relatively safe**, and because of this the interest amounts are usually low and the groups issuing bonds are normally solid. Because of their dependability, they are an important part of a diverse portfolio. By adding bonds to your portfolio, you can offset some of the risk of the stock market (see the next chapter).

You probably already know about U.S. Savings Bonds. You may already own some. These are considered by many to be the safest investments in the world, because the United States government is guaranteeing that your bond will be worth more in a few years than what you pay for it now. In the meantime, the government will use your money to make improvements in the country.

The interest that you earn on a bond depends on the federal interest rates. This means that, depending on when you buy a bond, the interest rate could be high or low. To get an idea of how bonds are doing, people normally watch a bond called the 30-Year Treasury Bond in the newspaper, on TV, or online. It is similar to the Dow Jones Industrial Average (see the section on stocks) in that it reflects the overall market.

Learn how to add bonds to your portfolio, go to **gotmoola.com**. There you'll find more information about specific bonds and how you can add them to your account.

EDUCATION AND COLLEGE

There are four other kinds of accounts that are designed to help you save for college. These accounts are perfect for the College Fund in your portfolio. Ask your parents or grandparents if they'll match funds with you, which means that for every dollar you put in, your relative will put the same amount into your account. Who knows, they might. But either way, you are going to benefit big time by opening one of these accounts soon.

Qualified Tuition Plans / 529 Plans

Qualified Tuition Plans (QTPs) are also known as Section 529 plans, or just 529 plans. These investment accounts are offered in most states. The great thing about these accounts is that you, a relative, or a friend can put away a lot of money in them. When you take out the money according to the rules, it's all tax-free! That doesn't mean that 529 plans are perfect.

There are two downsides to 529 Plans. The first is that because they are traded like a mutual fund (see the Investing Chapter) you cannot control how the money is invested. The second downside is that you can't take out your money whenever you want. If you take it out early, you will have to pay a penalty. The money is supposed to be withdrawn just for educational expenses. Also, they usually offer you only a few choices of what you can invest that money in.

Coverdell ESAs

With a Coverdell ESA account, you can invest up to $2,000 per year. Unlike a 529 plan, you have a lot more choices about how you invest the money in the account. You can invest it in whatever stocks, bonds or mutual funds that you'd like. When you withdraw money for qualified education expenses, it's tax-free. You can open a Coverdell ESA account through most brokerages and other financial institutions.

Since you never know exactly how much financial aid your preferred school(s) will offer you, having more money saved up is the best way to ensure that you can pay for college.

UGMAs and UTMAs

Finally, there are two kinds of special accounts, UGMAs and UTMAs. They're short for Uniform Gifts to Minors Act and Uniform Transfers to Minors Act. These are basically trusts, accounts set up by your parents or guardians. They become the trustee, investing money for you.

Once you are old enough (eighteen, twenty-one, or twenty-five depending on your area), the account becomes yours, and you can do with it what you want. Actually, it's been your property all along—you just aren't legally allowed to control it until a certain age.

Getting Parents in Gear...

Talking to your parents about college may seem a little weird right now. In fact, the idea of college may seem so far away that saving money for it sounds silly.

The problem is by the time you get to college, the cost of your education could cost as much as what your parents paid for their house!

Many of the accounts listed above can be opened without a minimum amount by your parents and can earn you money right away! Some of them, like a 529 account, let you earn money by doing the things you love, like shopping! You can learn more about these programs at *gotmoola.com*.

Bring your parents to your computer and show them the pages on setting up a college account. You might just teach them something!

Saving is the first big step in making your money **make** money. Your portfolio should always include a certain amount of savings. There are faster ways to grow your portfolio. Let's check them out...

Henry Ford

- Company: Ford Motor Co.®
- Detroit, Michigan

WHAT HE DID:

- Stayed true to his vision
- Adapted to meet the needs of his consumers

When he was only 16 years old, Henry Ford left his home on a farm to move to Detroit: Michigan's biggest city. He knew there was a lot to learn in Detroit and he had big ambitions. His first job was at the Detroit Dry Dock Company where they had an internal combustion engine. That's probably where he got his idea for building cars in a new way. Later, he got a job at Thomas Edison's company in Detroit testing new inventions. On his own time, Henry worked on something that looked like a car, but was really two bikes side-by-side with a small engine in between. Though it had the bad habit of breaking down in front of people he was trying to impress, he was still proud of his bike-car.

Five years later, Henry's newest car beat the world's fastest automobile in front of 8,000 people in Michigan. The money he made from that race helped him start the Ford Motor Company and in 1908 he built the Model T. He sold over 700,000 Model T's in just eight years. Henry Ford made a lot of money from his work on cars, but he also gave a lot of money away to people who weren't as lucky as he was. He built a hospital and started "The Ford Foundation." Since 1936, that foundation has given away more than $8 billion worldwide! Not bad for a farm boy.

BIZ WHIZ

Thomas Edison
- World Famous Inventor
- Milan, Ohio

WHAT HE DID:
- Recognized many underserved markets
- Persisted in the face of adversity

Thomas Edison invented the phonograph, the light bulb, and over 300 other things we use everyday. But before he was a famous inventor, he was just an ordinary kid with extraordinary ideas. When he was twelve, Thomas set up his first laboratory in their farm home's cellar. When Thomas was older he wrote and printed the "Grand Trunk Railroad Herald," a newspaper for the railroad employees. He printed the newspaper by himself on a small hand press and sold it to the 400 railroad workers. Soon thereafter, Thomas opened a laboratory to start working on ideas he had for other things people would like.

Even though Thomas had only three months of formal schooling, he knew education was important. Over the course of his life he read over 10,000 books and filled more than 25,000 notebooks with notes on his projects.

Thomas Edison is famous for his persistence. He would routinely run experiments a hundred times or more before having them go the way he hoped. Sometimes he would have over a thousand failures before he succeeded in his quest! Today, Thomas Edison is one of the most famous inventors of all time. His inventions are used every day by people like you. Just imagine: what if he had given up just because he made a few mistakes? Think of that the next time you turn on a light.

CHAPTER 5

INVESTING MONEY

A Money Tree is a fictional plant that, as it grows, continues to produce cash instead of leaves. A tree like that would need fertilizer, water, sun and, most importantly, your attention, to grow and bloom. Your portfolio is similar. To help ensure its growth, your portfolio should be diverse. We have discussed a number of methods of saving money in the previous chapter, including cash, savings accounts, and 529 accounts.

These methods are generally referred to as conservative investment methods. They have a **higher rate of security** and therefore normally have a **lower rate of return**. This means that while you can be relatively confident that your money will not depreciate or lower in value in these accounts, you also cannot expect a very fast increase in your money from these accounts.

INVESTING MONEY:

There are other ways of investing that can potentially be more lucrative. However, they will tend to be more risky as well. This is where you have to be smart and play the game wisely. Fortunes are made and lost every day on Wall Street and you want to be a long-term, stable winner.

REINVESTMENT

The saying "you have to spend money to make money" comes from the idea of reinvesting. Reinvestment can take many forms. If you choose to get employment with a company, you could reinvest in yourself by putting money towards your education.

The more education you have, the better you will be at your job or at running your own company. If you would like to start your own company, reinvestment is another word for growing your company. In order to grow your company you will need to spend some of your profit on additional supplies or help.

Maybe you need to hire a friend to increase the number of sales you can fill. Maybe you want to do some advertising for your company in the local newspaper. All of this costs money, but, if done wisely, could increase your overall earnings.

THE STOCK MARKET

OK! Now you have a front seat to one of the most exciting parts of the game! Give yourself a little time before you dive into stocks. You need to learn about them first and be smart about who ones you invest in.

The basics are simple. You want to choose companies that are profitable, well run and stable. You want to invest in good companies. When you invest in a good company, you are helping that company do even better and provide more jobs for people. You are helping the economy and you are helping our country. Investing in the stock market is investing in America, so choose wisely.

Every day, billions of dollars are spent on stocks around the world. These dollars are spent by people and institutions on companies listed on **Stock Exchanges**. These Stock Exchanges are there to guarantee that the companies listed with them have real assets and are legally registered to sell parts of themselves to the public via slips of paper called stock. If you have 100 percent of the stock, you own the entire company.

However, many huge corporations are controlled by people with much less. For example, Bill Gates controls Microsoft™, though he owns far less than half of the stock.

When you buy a stock in a company, you are in effect giving them money to keep doing what they do. In exchange you will get some tiny portion of the profits for each piece of stock you buy.

INVESTING MONEY:

ONE GIANT MYTH

"Young People Can Afford to Take High Risk"

Of all the myths in the stock market, this may be the cruelest and the most foolish! Everyone knows that the elderly are not supposed to take risks. They must be very conservative because their earning power is limited. They can't afford to lose their money! Well, who decided that young people could afford to lose their money?

If any group needed to watch every penny, it's the young. **YOU!** One day you will need money to start a family, buy a house, buy furniture, start a business, save for the future and on and on. Furthermore, the younger you are, the higher the likelihood you are going to be at the lower end of the earning scale. That's just the way it goes. You have to be careful with every cent you make.

However, **YOU** have a super asset on your side. **TIME!** You have time. You don't need to take big risks financially. You can invest in tried-and-true companies that make money year in and year out. At 10 percent per year growth, your investments will double every seven years. By the time most people are just starting out, you can have the down payment for your own recording studio or house. When you have time, you get to have patience. Patience pays off in the stock market.

 When you enter the world of stocks, you are taking chances that you need to be aware of. Before you open an account to buy and sell stocks you need to get your parents' permission. You also need to get the best advice possible.

HOW TO PICK STOCKS

If you go in to any decent bookstore or library, you'll find shelves full of books on how to pick stocks. Not all them are useful. It isn't easy, but sorting out the good stuff from the not-so-good stuff is absolutely necessary.

The biggest obstacle to finding a winning stock picking system is that no system works all the time. Nevertheless, there are some simple, common sense rules that can improve anyone's stock picking skills, regardless of the system they use.

Here are some rules you need to keep in mind:

1. FAVOR UNDERVALUED STOCKS

- The first step in picking stocks is to favor stocks of companies that are making money, lots of money. Study stocks of companies with rapidly growing earnings, and choose stocks of companies that consistently make more money than they did the year before.

- These stocks usually sell at very high prices, however, if their Value is more than the Price, they're still a good bargain. Determining a company's value is not simple. You need information.

2. FAVOR SAFE STOCKS

- You will notice that the prices of certain major companies tend to cause little excitement, though they go up year after year. Others, are always in the news, and go up and down consistently.

- The reason is simple. The former have track records of steady earning performance, while the latter has an erratic earnings record.

  Price volatility (craziness) is known as the roller-coaster effect and comes about due to fear and uncertainty.

3. FAVOR STOCKS WITH RISING PRICES

- Don't try and pick the bottom of the market.
  Pick a rising trend.

- You never know where the bottom (the smallest amount a stock will be worth) is when buying a stock whose price is falling.

- A stock that is rising in price is already doing what you want it to do.

Don't worry if this seems a bit confusing now. Stocks just have a few more rules than most parts of the game of making money. Keep reading and you'll be teaching your parents about stocks! You can also go to *gotmoola.com* for a stock analysis of companies that you're interested in.

THE ROLLER-COASTER EFFECT

Expect the prices of shares to go up and down when you invest in shares of stock. They will, every day, sometimes for understandable reasons, sometimes for no apparent reason. On the next two pages list some of the many reasons why a stock price will move up or down.

Why Stocks Go Up...

- A great review or flattering coverage in the media
- Increasing sales and profits
- The company lands a big new contract
- The company wins a lawsuit
- The company expands globally and starts selling in other countries
- Scientists discover something important
- A famous investor or celebrity is buying shares
- A great new executive is hired to run the company
- An exciting new product or service is introduced
- An analyst upgrades the company, for instance, from "buy" to "strong buy"
- Other stocks in the same industry go up
- A competitor's company goes out of business
- More people are buying the product or service
- The industry is "hot"—people expect big things for good reasons
- The industry is "hot"—people don't understand much about it, but they're buying anyway
- The company is bought by another company
- The company is going to "spin-off" part of itself as a new company
- Rumors
- Just because

Why Stocks Go Down

- Profits and/or sales begin to slip
- Another company comes out with a better product
- There's a supply shortage, so not enough of the product can be made
- A big lawsuit is filed against the company
- Scientists discover the product is not safe
- Fewer people are buying the product
- Other stocks in the same industry go down
- Most of the stock market is down
- The industry used to be "hot," but now another industry is more popular
- Top executives leave the company
- A famous investor sells shares of the company
- An analyst downgrades their recommendation of the stock, maybe from "buy" to "hold"
- The company loses a major customer
- Some new law might hurt sales or profits
- A powerful company becomes a competitor
- Rumors
- Just because

Can you think of any other reasons why a stock would go up or down? If so, go ahead and add them to the list.

A Piece of the Pie...

Pick a company from the list below. Using today's newspaper, write down the stock's price. You can find the price of the stock by looking for its index name (example Coca-Cola™ is listed under the New York Stock Exchange as "KO").

Each day for a week write down the price of the stock. You will see it move up and down. If there is a big change, try to find out if the company was in the news that day. Look at the list of reasons why the price can change. See if you can guess why the change happened.

SOME DIVIDEND PAYING COMPANIES

Coca-Cola (NYSE: KO), PepsiCo (NYSE: PEP), Abercrombie & Fitch (NYSE: ANF), Starbucks (Nasdaq: SBUX), Apple Computer (Nasdaq: AAPL), Dell Computer (Nasdaq: DELL), Microsoft (Nasdaq: MSFT), Intel (Nasdaq: INTC), AOL Time Warner (NYSE: AOL), Ford Motor Company (NYSE: F), General Motors (NYSE: GM), Boeing (NYSE: BA), Nike (NYSE: NKE), Callaway Golf (NYSE: ELY), Wal-Mart (NYSE: WMT), Home Depot (NYSE: HD), Scholastic (Nasdaq: SCHL), Viacom (NYSE: VIA), ExxonMobil (NYSE: XOM), McDonald's (NYSE: MCD), Wendy's (NYSE: WEN),

INVESTING MONEY:

CHANGE SHOULD BE EXPECTED

The change in a stock's price from day to day is called volatility. Stocks that go up and down a lot during a day are considered to be more volatile than those that change only a little. Volatile stocks are often in fast-changing industries or those that are dependent on technology or hot areas.

These companies' stocks can change many times each day. These changes can add up over time, with a volatile stock moving up and down by large percentages. This kind of movement can scare investors. However, the smart investor realizes that volatility is just part of the game. Let's look at an hexample of a stock that has been volatile. Let's see what we can learn from it.

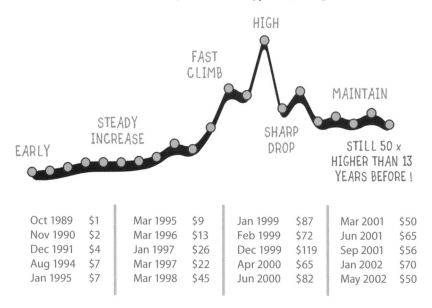

COMPANY STOCK PRICES

Oct 1989	$1	Mar 1995	$9	Jan 1999	$87	Mar 2001	$50
Nov 1990	$2	Mar 1996	$13	Feb 1999	$72	Jun 2001	$65
Dec 1991	$4	Jan 1997	$26	Dec 1999	$119	Sep 2001	$56
Aug 1994	$7	Mar 1997	$22	Apr 2000	$65	Jan 2002	$70
Jan 1995	$7	Mar 1998	$45	Jun 2000	$82	May 2002	$50

This kind of chart shows that while there has been a lot of change in the company's stock price over the last few years, people who held on to their stock for five or more years made money. The point is not to worry too much about the volatility of a stock in the short term. Assuming you bought the stock for a good reason—and you still have faith in the company—patience should pay off.

DIVERSIFY

Just like it's a good idea to keep your portfolio diverse, it's a good idea to keep your brokerage account diverse. Remember Dr. Bart DiLiddo? He's also a leading investment counselor. Here's what he has to say about diversity in your account:

"It pays to diversify. That old saw about putting your eggs in a single basket and watching it carefully makes no sense for the average investor. There are just too many uncontrolled variables in the stock market. Moreover, the average investor is the last to hear about bad news when it hits.

I recommend that investors reduce risk by diversifying. This may be done by investing in a variety of different stocks in different industries, and by investing over a period of time. Don't plunge into the market all at one time.

The amount of money to put into any single stock depends, of course, upon your personal circumstances. As a rule of thumb, I like to see between ten and twenty stocks in a portfolio. Invest approximately equal dollar amounts into each of the stocks you buy. This is called **dollar weighting**. It ties in with reducing risk by diversifying. While diversification is good, too much diversification will dilute your portfolio's performance and add to commission costs."

THE ALL-STAR LISTS

Just like in sports, there are all-star stocks. These stocks are chosen by various established groups and placed in a list called an index. There are many different indexes and index funds (funds that track the index lists). The three most famous indexes are:

- **The Dow Jones Industrial Average (TOTAL COMPANIES: 30)**
  "The Dow" is an index of thirty of the biggest companies in America, such as McDonald's, Coca-Cola, General Electric, and Microsoft. This is the most famous index. It's also the oldest index, having started more than 100 years ago.

- **The S&P 500 (TOTAL COMPANIES: 500)**
  This is an index of 500 companies that are among the biggest and best companies in America. Just about any major company you can think of is in the S&P 500. The S&P 500 is often used as a benchmark for the entire stock market. In other words, if the S&P 500 rises 3 percent, people will say that the market has risen 3 percent.

  S&P 500 Companies include: Ford, Motorola, Dell, Apple, McDonald's, Coca-Cola, Microsoft, Intel, Cisco, eBay, Jostens, Hershey, Maytag, Hasbro, Gillette, Staples, Toys R Us, Sprint, Fruit of the Loom, Radio Shack, Wal-Mart... and many more!

- **The Wilshire 5000 (TOTAL COMPANIES: more than 7000)**
  If you want to see how the market is really doing, the Wilshire 5000 is a good place to check. Once there were only about 5,000 companies that sold stock. At that time the Wilshire 5000 index contained almost all of them. That's how it got its name. Today the index contains more than 7,000 companies, but it's name stays the same. The Wilshire 5000 is often referred to as the "total market" index.

Indexes help people get a sense of how a group of companies is doing or how the market is doing as a whole. They are used as standards for people to compare their own stocks against. There are many indexes and for each of the big indexes, like the ones listed, there is a fund that invests in the companies on the list. This means that if you buy into that fund, like a Wilshire 5000 index fund, you are also buying a small piece of each of its 7000 companies. Pretty cool, huh?

FUN WITH FUNDS

What happens when you only have a small amount to invest? What happens if you're worried about picking the wrong stock? Should you put your money in a CD or bank account earning very little interest, or maybe none at all? Maybe. But there are other options. **EXCITING OPTIONS!** They're called **funds**.

Imagine if you could pool your money with a group of friends. Let's say that you and 10 friends each invested $500 into one account. With that $5000, you can earn more money and have more options available to you. You can diversify and create a much more balanced portfolio.

That's basically what a fund is, expect that instead of 10 people, most funds have thousands (or tens of thousands) of investors. Instead of $5,000, the typical fund is worth millions or billions of dollars. While the average investor who invests on their own might hold stock in just eight to fifteen companies, the typical mutual fund will hold shares in more than 100 companies!

INVESTING MONEY:

FUND FINDING

There are lots of funds to choose from when you invest. The good news is that most of them fall under three categories:

- **Money market funds**: A money market fund buys CDs and bonds issued by the government or companies. Because of this, Money Market Funds are generally safe, but don't perform as well as other funds.

- **Fixed-income funds**: These funds generally invest in bonds.

- **Equity funds**: "Equity" is the same as saying "stock." Equity funds invest in stocks.

Typically, you'll earn the most with stock funds. Bond funds are next, then money market funds which generally earn less than bond funds and stock funds. For more information on them, check out *gotmoola.com*.

MAYBE NOT FOR YOU

Mutual funds do have their advantages. They're certainly convenient, especially if you don't know much about investing. They give you instant diversification. It would be risky to have all your money invested in just one or two companies, but with mutual funds, you're usually in more than 100 companies (or other investments) at once.

There are some considerable disadvantages though:

- **The majority perform worse than the market average.** This is referred to as underperforming. In fact, more than 75 percent of stock mutual funds do worse than the overall stock market. Not a very good way to make money.

- **Most funds do too much buying and selling.** This is called turnover, or "churning." It's bad because each time you (or a mutual fund) buys or sells something, a commission is charged. The commission charges can really add up. Also, every time a stock is sold with earnings, taxes must be paid on that stock. Guess who pays the taxes? You do.

- **Mutual funds can be too big to do well.** Some have more than $10 billion invested in them. That means that it's hard for them to find good investments. To counter this, some funds invest in hundreds of companies. Remember when we said diversity is good? Like most things, that's true in moderation. Funds that invest in too many companies are less likely to perform well because the winners and losers cancel each other out.

- **Mutual funds often charge high fees.** These fees are called loads and they are taken out of your money! If you invest in a mutual fund that charges a 5 percent load and you invest $2,000, they will take out $100 as their fee. That means you're really only investing $1,900. If you want to try mutual funds, be sure to look for one that offers no-load investment.

Can you name five other kinds of investing
that we have talked about?

INVESTING MONEY:

IT'S NOT MUTUAL – IT'S AN INDEX

Index funds can save you from the problems with mutual funds that we just talked about. Index funds automatically invest in all of the companies that are associated with a particular index (like the S&P 500). This has many advantages.

The first might seem kind of funny. Compared with mutual funds that generally do worse than average, index funds often perform, well... average. Maybe not exciting, but it's a lot better than doing **worse** than average. Index funds are generally cheaper than mutual funds. Index funds usually sport extremely low fees, sometimes much less than 1 percent. Lastly, there's normally little turnover within index funds. They hold stock in whatever companies are in their index list.

 Index investing may not be as exciting as picking your own individual stocks, but it will get the job done and over time should make you more money.

AVERAGE ISN'T ALWAYS BAD

Index funds should be considered relatively stable long-term funds. If you buy shares in them you should expect to hang on to them for at least ten years. The performance of these indexes is often said to be "average". That means that the money that you have invested in index funds will go up and down at about the same rate as the U.S. economy. This isn't a bad thing. You could invest only in index funds and still do better than most people who don't invest. However, if you want to make more than the average you'll need to look at individual stocks and other methods of investing.

READER/CUSTOMER CARE SURVEY

We care about your opinions. Please take a moment to fill out this Reader Survey card and mail it back to us.

As a special **"thank you"** we'll send you exciting news about interesting books and a valuable **Gift Certificate.**

Please PRINT using ALL CAPS

Name First _____ MI. _____ Last Name _____

Address _____

City _____ ST _____ Zip _____

Phone # (_____) _____ — _____ Fax # (_____) _____ — _____

Email _____

(1) Gender:
_____ Female _____ Male

(2) Age:
_____ 8 or younger _____ 17-20
_____ 9-12 _____ 21-30
_____ 13-16 _____ 31+

(3) What attracts you most to a book?
(Please rank 1-4 in order of preference.)

	1	2	3	4
6) Content	○	○	○	○
5) Author	○	○	○	○
4) Cover Design	○	○	○	○
3) Title	○	○	○	○

(7) Other than school books, how many books do you read a month?
_____ 1 _____ 3
_____ 2 _____ 4

(8) How did you find out about this book?
Please fill in ONE.
1) _____ Friend
2) _____ School (Teacher, Library, etc.)
3) _____ Parent
4) _____ Store Display
5) _____ Teen Magazine
6) _____ Interview/Review (TV, Radio, Print)

(9) Where do you usually buy books?
Please fill in your top TWO choices.
1) _____ Bookstore
2) _____ Religious Bookstore
3) _____ Online
4) _____ Book Club/Mail Order
5) _____ Price Club (Costco, Sam's Club, etc.)
6) _____ Retail Store (Target, Wal-Mart, etc.)

(11) Did you receive this book as a gift?
_____ Yes _____ No

(12) What do you like to read? *(Please check all that apply)*

Magazines:
12) _____ Teen People
13) _____ Seventeen
14) _____ YM
15) _____ Cosmo Girl
16) _____ Rolling Stone
17) _____ Teen Ink
18) _____ Christian Magazines

Books:
19) _____ Fiction
20) _____ Self/Help Books
21) _____ Reality Stories/Memoirs
22) _____ Sports
23) _____ Series Books (Chicken Soup, Fearless, etc.)

TAPE IN MIDDLE; DO NOT STAPLE

BUSINESS REPLY MAIL

FIRST-CLASS MAIL PERMIT NO 45 DEERFIELD BEACH, FL

POSTAGE WILL BE PAID BY ADDRESSEE

HCI TEENS
3201 SW 15TH STREET
DEERFIELD BEACH FL 33442-9875

I₁ıIIıııIIIıIıIıIIıIıIıIIIIıIıIıIıIıııIıIıIıIıI

FOLD HERE

(24) Do you prefer to read books written by:

1) _____ Teen Authors?

2) _____ Adult Authors?

3) _____ No Preference

Comments:

Mary McLeod Bethune

- Company: Bethune-Cookman
  College
- Daytona, Florida

WHAT SHE DID:

- Stayed true to her vision

The key ingredient to economic success has always been education. In the American South in the late 1800s there were very few educational opportunities for Americans of African descent. One girl found this appalling and decided to do something about it.

Mary McLeod Bethune was very bright and was able to get a scholarship to schools in the North where she studied extremely hard. However, her heart broke for other children down in the south still barred from school because of their color. In 1904 Mary decided to do something about it and she opened a first school in Daytona, Florida. She had five students and she called it the Daytona Literary and Industrial School for Training Negro Girls. Mary was a very strong woman who knew how to inspire her students to do their best.

She also knew how to inspire people to donate money so that the school could grow. Year by year the school grew; first into a high school, then a junior college, and she didn't stop until it became the Bethune-Cookman College. Mary never allowed other people to crush her dreams, nor did she allow limitations to control her destiny. Remarkably, Mary began her school with only $1.50 to her name. Just think what she could have done with ten bucks.

P.T. Barnum

- Company: Barnum & Bailey's
  Circus and Museums
- Showman, Entrepreneur, Optomist

WHAT HE DID:

- Reinvented himself
- Identified needs of consumer

He was America's second millionaire, one of the greatest promoters of all time, beloved by his employees and a leading fighter for the freedom of slaves who lost his entire fortune at the age of 46 only to build a new one that was even larger! Phineas Taylor Barnum was born in 1810 and is most famous for creating the Barnum & Bailey Circus which still exists.

P.T. Barnum is often quoted as saying "There's a sucker born every minute." However, he never said that. In fact, Barnum believed in giving his customers a great show at a great price. He also believed in advertising and was a phenomenal promoter. He once used an elephant to plow a field next to a railroad because he knew that all of the people on the trains going by would want to come back and see the elephant in his circus.

P.T. Barnum faced great adversity in his life but never lost his optimistic spirit. Even when his beloved home burnt down and he lost his fortune he quickly rebuilt them both. He is one of the most incredible entrepreneurs of all time who was beloved by both his employees and the public.

TAXES AND MORE FUNDS

Just like Uncle Sam takes a bite out of your paycheck, your stocks and funds are subject to being taxed as well. The good news is that by understanding the basics, you can avoid paying more in taxes than is necessary. For example, let's say that you have invested in shares of Coca-Cola™ stock. Four times a year Coca-Cola pays you a dividend based on their earnings. Those dividends count as taxable income so you will need to report them on your tax return.

When you sell your stock, taxes will also come into play. If you sell your shares for less than you paid for them, you will have a capital loss. You want to make sure to report this on your tax return because you will get to deduct that amount from your income, up to $3,000. For example, if you earned $5,000 during the year but had $1,000 in losses from selling your stock, it is as if you only earned $4,000. This means your taxes may be lower.

The opposite is true if you make money when you sell your stock. If you sell your stock for more than you paid, you will have a capital gain. Capital gain is considered taxable income and must be reported.

The length of time you own a stock will, in part, determine how much you pay in taxes on that capital gain. If you held on to the stock for a year or less, the tax rate is the same as your general income tax. However, if you held it for longer than a year then it becomes a long-term gain. Long-term gains are taxed at rates that are lower than most people's income tax rate. All the more reason to be aware of how long you've had a stock when you decide to sell it.

If you sell shares in more than one stock in a year you may be able to offset your gains with your losses. Like the example, if your gains were $5,000 and you reported losses of $1,000 then you only gained $4,000. This would be the amount that would be taxable.

Mutual funds are subject to taxing as well. If you sell shares of your fund, you will have a gain or a loss. If your fund contains stocks that pay dividends, that amount will also be taxable.

If you have questions about what is or isn't taxable, you can always ask your broker or investment manager. You might want to ask them about other types of accounts that aren't subject to taxes in the same way. We'll go over some of these next.

IRAS: TRADITIONAL AND ROTH

One kind of account you can open when you open your brokerage account is called an IRA. **An IRA is a retirement account**. It is designed for investments people make for when they are much older and are considering retiring. The money you put in an IRA shouldn't be removed until you are in your sixties. Why would you want that? One big reason is that using an IRA can help you pay less in taxes!

Many banks, brokerages, mutual fund companies and other financial firms will let you open an IRA with your brokerage account (with your parents there). Because IRAs can help you in paying your taxes, you can only put money that you've earned into an IRA. That means that gifts don't count. You need to put either money you've earned through your job, your company or through interest into the IRA. Also, there are limits to how much you can put into an IRA. For 2002, the limit is $3,000. There are two main kinds of IRAs: Traditional and Roth.

• **A Traditional IRA** is one in which you can store pre-tax money. The money you invest gets to grow in a tax-deferred manner. This means that you can buy and sell stocks or funds in your account and can generate capital gains, but you're not taxed on them (for now). You won't have to pay those taxes until you start taking your money out at retirement. But, if you try to withdraw the money before you are old enough, you will get fined.

• **In a Roth IRA**, you invest post-tax money. When you are at retirement age, you can start taking the money out tax free! Here's how it works. You don't get a tax break up front, as you would with the traditional IRA. Instead, you get the tax break when you withdraw the funds. It's a big break and can mean that you save a lot of money!

It can be hard to imagine yourself retiring. It can be hard to imagine being 25! So this might not seem that exciting. But remember that you don't have to put every dollar you earn into an IRA. For most teens, the Roth IRA is the best choice. Imagine, you might be the first teen at your school with both a Roth IRA account and a regular brokerage account! Don't let anyone tell you that a minor isn't allowed to start an IRA! Anyone of any age can, as long as it's with earned income.

There are so many different kinds of investment accounts! Don't get confused. It just means there are many options for you. Try starting with an index fund and see where your interests take you.

IT CAN BE COOL TO BE A DRIP!

You should check out investing in "Drips." That's the nickname for Dividend Reinvestment Plans (DRPs) or direct investment plans. A Drip allows you to buy shares of a company's stock directly from the company, skipping brokerages and their commissions. More than 1000 companies currently offer this service. sBack when brokerage commissions could be $50 or $100 or more per trade, this would save you a lot of money.

Now with some bargain brokerages charging $8 or less per trade, this benefit isn't as big. The real benefit of Drips comes into play with dividends. With a Drip you can have your dividends reinvested into additional shares of the stock automatically.

This means that if you earn $10 in dividends and the company's stock is selling at $20, you can purchase a half share of the stock with the dividend. Normally you can't buy half shares but through Drips you can. Now that's cool!

Some Drips require that you already own a share of the stock before you can sign up for the plan (kind of a pain). See if you can find a company you like that allows you to buy your first share through the Drip. For some help getting started with Drips go to *gotmoola.com*.

Estee Lauder

- Company: Estee Lauder®
- New York City, New York

WHAT SHE DID:

- Identified a new market
- Combined her interests with sales innovation

Estee Lauder is a name that you may recognize. The company that still bears her name is worth billions of dollars and is a huge success. However, it did not start out that way. Estee Lauder was born Josephine Esther Mentzer in New York City. Her parents were immigrants who ran a hardware store that they lived above. Josephine started her first business ventures by selling creams for the skin that her uncle made. He was a chemist who knew how to create potions that Josephine would sell in beauty shops and at resorts.

Josephine, who began calling herself Estee, was extremely serious about making sure everything she sold was of the highest quality. But as good as the creams and potions were, her ability to sell was even better. Estee also worked very hard. She would keep after a potential customer until they finally gave in and bought her products. Her big break came in 1948 when she was able to start selling her perfumes and creams at Saks Fifth Avenue. The wealthy customers loved Estee's products and the personable way in which she sold them. Estee told them all of the benefits they would receive by using her line of products. As she began to sell her products to more stores, she would personally go to each one and train the people. She would show them how to treat a customer. This proved to be a huge success and today, you can find Estee Lauder products around the world.

DOUBLE TAKE...
Can you solve the mystery?

A policeman holds a cocky thief in handcuffs as a bank president walks out to his parking lot. A young mother stands nearby, comforting her toddler. She says that she'd come to make a deposit in her baby's new college fund. But when she turned to get her daughter out of the car the thief snuck up, grabbed her wallet and ran. Luckily he ran right into the policeman. The policeman opens the wallet and he finds a deposit slip and $25 in cash. He frowns and the thief laughs. The woman asks whats wrong and the policeman says that unfortunately, in their town, you have to steal at least $100 in order to get jail time. The bank president steps forward and suggests to the thief that he stop laughing for he had in fact stolen $100.

Why had he stolen $100?

Answer – Because the woman was on bank property with a deposit slip and cash for her little daughters college account. By the time the girl reached eighteen and withdrew the money for college – that deposit would be worth over $100. So, that in fact is how much was stolen from the little girl.

THE IDEA HATCHER

You are about to come up with an idea. Moola will guide you through the game. This will be an idea for your idea bank. Get ready. In fifteen minutes you may have something you want to do that you never even dreamed of. Or you may have something absolutely silly. Great accomplishments always start with an idea. So when you're ready, *GET SET* and *GO!*

You will have **15 minutes** to **draw, write, doodle, diagram** and **dream** your way to the idea that's going to hatch out of the Idea Egg below. Just think, in the next 15 minutes you could come up with an idea that could change the world or one that's just plain silly, or both.

You Will Need:
Pen or Pencil
This Book
Watch/Clock/Timer

IDEA
EGG

At the end of the game you will crack the Idea Egg and see what comes out… Whatever pops in your mind is what you put down.

Picture an egg in your mind and on the shell it has the words "I LIKE" written on it. Inside there is a piece of paper with a word on it. This word completes the sentence "I like ____." Look at that word in your mind. What is that word? Write that word, now.

 Write that word here. Don't think. Just write...

_____

Now take the first three letters in that word and write three new words that start with those letters and are things you like about the first word in your egg. **For example**: If your word is **Basketball**, you could write...

BASKETBALL

Buddies   Athleticism   Strategy

② Now write your final three words down.
They also go in your egg...

_____

_____

_____

EXTRAORDINARY!

LET'S KEEP GOING...

Switch your thinking and do a three line drawing. Each line represents one of your three related words. Don't worry about being a great artist, this is about letting go. Close your eyes and think of the first of your three related words and draw a quick two inch line on the paper. Next, close your eyes and draw a line representing the second word. It can represent how it looks or how it feels to you. That's right, feels.

Let the emotion guide the motion. Now, draw the third line. Close your eyes and do it now. Great.

 Just start drawing...

Time to clean up your act. Now, draw all three lines again, this time with your eyes open. You can clean them up and reposition them a bit. But all three have to stay within a two inch by two inch box. After you finish your redraw, do a real small version inside your egg on page 135.

Go for it...

OK, you are over halfway there. You now need to make a sentence that includes all four of the words in your egg. The sentence starts with the words... "I will" and in the middle it has the words... "because it will". You can add as many words as you like. Let's go back to the "basketball" example. The other three words are... 'buddies', 'athletes' and 'strategy'. The sentence could look like this...

For example: "I will play **strategic basketball** with **buddies** that are **athletes** because it will make me healthier and happier."

Notice that we changed 'strategy' to 'strategic'. You can change the words like that to make your sentence work.

(4) Now it's your turn:

I will... _____

_____

because it will... _____

_____

With that done, write at least three things you will need to accomplish what you've written you will do.

For example to play basketball you'd need: A Basketball, Players and Shoes plus you might want a bottle of water or a jersey.

(5) Go ahead and list them...

_____

_____

_____

(6) Circle the one you could figure out how to make. Write it in your egg.

Now, from all the words in your egg—pick three of them that sound good together. Don't worry whether or not they make sense.

For example: "Buddies Play Basketball."

(7) Go ahead and list them here...

_____

_____

_____

(8) These three words go in your egg.
They'd probably look good on a sticker.

That's it my friend, you are ready to hatch an idea from your egg! You can use the egg on the next page.

YOU DID IT!

You can use the egg below to keep track of the steps from the previous pages. To start over go to **page 129**:

1) Your First
   Word

2) Three Related
   Words

3) Three Line
   Drawing

4) Your "I will"
   Sentence

5) Three Things
   You Need

6) The Thing You
   Can Make

7) Three
   Words Go
   Together

Now let's take this egg and wrap up what we know about your company. You'll be surprised what kind of cool things can come out of your egg.

135

MY NEW BUSINESS IDEA

My company is (#7): _____

I make (#6): _____

My logo is (#3):

My friend, you have just hatched an idea!

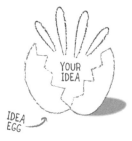

YOUR
IDEA

IDEA
EGG

You can put this idea of yours in your **Idea Bank** to consider later, or you can act on it right now. You can repeat this exercise any time you want on a blank sheet of paper, or in the back of the book. When you have an idea that you want to act upon, you'll need a plan. That's what we'll do next. Check it out. **It's wild!**

BUSINESS PLAN BRAINSTORM
WHO SAYS MONEY DOESN'T GROW ON TREES?

WELCOME TO THE JUNGLE! It's wild in here. If you look around you'll find that money literally grows on trees. You just need a map to keep you on the right path. The trick is the path keeps twisting and changing. But that's part of what makes it so fun. It's also why you need a guide like Moola.

Your business needs a map too, this map is called a **Business Plan**. Business Plans can be complex or very simple but they all do basically the same thing—keep the business on the right path. All you need to do is follow Moola's directions below. If you don't know any of the first answers, flip back and play **Crack the Egg** and you'll know what to write.

1. Write your Company name: _____

2. Write what you make: _____

3. Draw your logo:

In one line tell Moola what you are going to be selling. For example, mowing a lawn is a service. A scarf is a product. Both are kinds of sales. In both cases somebody pays you money in exchange for an item or service.

(4) I am going to be charging $ _____

in exchange for _____

Are you doing this alone or with someone else. If you have partners write their names here:

_____

_____

Whether you have invented a new make-up applicator, or you're baby-sitting kids, people will pay you because they want or need what you are offering. Let's write it out…

(5) People will pay me because they want or need :

_____

_____

_____

Now that we know what you want to do and how much you'll charge, let's think about the best ways of building your business. Being smart about money as you start, will payoff big as your company grows.

Whether you're selling world class athletic skills to a pro-sports team or custom tie-dyed socks in your school's colors, the initial planning all breaks down to a couple simple questions.

(6) Can you buy your finished product from someone else and if so how much will it cost?

_____

(7) If you are going to make your product yourself, what do you need to make it and how much will each part cost?

_____

_____

(8) How long will it take you to purchase what you need and get the final product or service to your first customer?

_____

(9) Write down what it will cost you to do this? The difference between this and the number you put for number 6 or number 7, is your Profit.

_____

_____

(10) Who is the one person you are most sure will pay you for your product?

_____

(11) Put at least one more possible sales target down. It may be a neighbor, a friend, your parents, or perhaps business people in an office nearby...

_____

_____

(12) Write down four things you plan to accomplish in the next week. They should be associated with the words starting each line...

Research _____

Production _____

Promotion _____

Sales _____

YOU DID IT! You've created your first business plan! Get started, you have a busy week in front of you. To find out more about business plans, visit *gotmoola.com*

CONGRATULATIONS!!!

You have the info you need!   You have the power to succeed!
Let's run through a quick game plan based on what we discussed in the book. Following this advice, being determined and working hard is the best way to guarantee that you make more than your parents and achieve your goals.

1) Remember the goal of the game: Financial Freedom.

2) The key to the game is making your money work for you.

3) Set your goals and review them often to see how you are doing.

4) Know that you are a highly capable and unique person.

5) Be alert to opportunities while doing the things you love.

6) Each day, visit with others just like you at the web site *gotmoola.com*.

SOON YOU'LL BE MAKING MORE THAN YOUR PARENTS!
SEE YOU ONLINE!

USE THE FOLLOWING PAGES TO LOOK UP
MORE INFORMATION AND WRITE DOWN
YOUR BRILLIANT IDEAS AS YOU
HEAD DOWN THE PATH TO SUCCESS!

Take a banana
for the road...

Still hungry for more? Check out these great books and games for additional information about the topics we discussed in this book. Visit us on the Web at ***gotmoola.com*** to order them at a special price!

Dollarville
PC Game

by Magnetic Entertainment

Dollarville is a wild western adventure game that guides young investors through the land of Dollarville. Learn what it takes to be money smart while having fun. Available now on ***gotmoola.com.***

How to Get a Job If You're a Teenager

by Cindy Pervola and Debby Hobgood

This book provides a simple recipe on how you, or any young adult for that matter, can go about getting a job. The text includes a basic job skills guide with appendices of additional resources and Web sites for job searches.

Complete Idiot's Guide to Cool Jobs for Teens

by Susan Ireland

Finding the right job can make all the difference. In the standard *Idiot's Guide* fashion, *The Complete Idiot's Guide to Cool Jobs for Teens* teaches job-finding skills and confidence boosting. It also discusses resumes and cover letter writing, interviewing techniques, job-keeping skills, being an entrepreneur, spending and saving on a salary and exploring internships and volunteering.

143

The 7 Habits of Highly Effective Teens
by Sean Covey

The *7 Habits* series has been helping adults in the business world for years. With this book, author Sean Covey provides a step-by-step guide to help you improve self-image, build friendships, resist peer pressure, achieve goals, get along with your parents, and more. In *The 7 Habits of Highly Effective Teens,* Covey applies the timeless principles of the *7 Habits* to teens and the tough issues and life-changing decisions you face every day.

Cool Careers for Dummies
by Marty Nemko and Paul and Sarah Edwards

Looking for a job? Worried about making the right choice? *Cool Careers for Dummies* can not only help you find a job you never knew existed, but make it fun! There are sections on resumes, interviews, and salary negotiation, making this the a useful guide if you are a first-time job hunter or a seasoned professional looking for a change.

100 Best Careers for the 21st Century
by Shelly Field

This book is for career hunters of all ages. In fact, your parents should probably read this when you're done! By examining the hot jobs of today, Shelly Field's guide to careers of the 21st century is a great, practical place to start the process of matching your interests and skills with the job market.

The Teenager's Guide to the Real World
by Marshall Brain

Starting from the idea that you should be able to design your own life, this book was written to help you see the amazing freedom you have to control your life and destiny. It then attempts to help you make good decisions about the future. Many of the choices that you make as a teenager will affect you for the rest of your life! After reading this book you'll hopefully understand more about yourself and the world around you.

Discover What You're Best At
by Linda Gale

The unique career aptitude system in this book helps you to identify not only your interests but also your innate talents and potential skills. Once you have a better idea about what you're best at, match your career strengths to dozens of the more than 1,100 jobs described in detail. Let the hunt begin!

A Kid's Guide to Money
by Steve Otfinoski

Tons of useful facts and wise suggestions about managing your money are organized and presented in a straight-forward and fun way. The section on operating a business will be great if you are entrepreneurial and already have a venture in mind.

If you're still craving more, here are some additional books worth checking out. When you're done reading them, visit the *gotmoola.com* Web site and share your thoughts:

The Totally Awesome Money Book for Kids and Their Parents
Author: Berg, Adrienne G.
NY: Newmarket Press, 1993

Dr. Tightwad's Money-Smart Kids, 2nd ed.
Author: Bodnar, Janet
Washington, D.C.: New York
Kiplinger Books ; Times Business, 1997.

Kiplinger's Money-Smart Kids
Author: Bodnar, Janet
Washington, D.C. : Kiplinger Books, 1993.

Fast Cash for Kids
Author: Drew, Bonnie J., & Drew, O. Noel
TX: Homeland Publishing, 1987

Kids, Money & Values
Author: Estess, Patricia Schiff
OH: Betterway Books, 1994.

Cash University Course Kit
Author: Stawski, Willard S., II
MI: Cash University, 1998.

WORDS TO KNOW

Looking for a particular word or idea? This book is full of them! Here's a list in alphabetical order of terms for your reference. Use this area if you forget what a word means, how it's used or what else relates to it:

A

Account
A virtual file with a company like a bank or brokerage firm that contains money that they are either holding or investing for you.

B

Brokerage
Company that buys and sells stocks for clients, like you.

Brokerage Account
Your stock account that you maintain with a brokerage firm.

C

Capital Gain
Selling your shares of stock for more than you paid for them.

Capital Loss
Selling your shares of stock for less than you paid for them.

Career Growth Plan
Strategy to increase your skill set and income in an industry that you find to be interesting.

Client
Someone who purchases your product or service.

Comparison Shopping
Doing research on the best deals before purchasing products and services.

Conservative
A method of investing money that is low-risk and typically has a lower rate of return.

Customer
Someone who purchases your product or service.

D

Deduct
Subtract or remove.

Demand
Consumer need or motivation for a product or service.

Depreciate
Lower in value.

Dividend
Bonus or payment.

E

Earning Potential
The amount of money you will most likely earn in the future compared to the amount you are earning now.

Education
Constant pursuit of knowledge, gained from books, experience, school, people, and life in general.

Educational Fund
An account or series of accounts that finance your education.

Employee
A person that has been hired by a company or individual to do a job or service. Hired by an employer.

Employer
The hiring person or company that pays workers to complete tasks. Hires employees.

Entrepreneurship
Being your own boss and creating a company or service of your own.

F

Financial Freedom
Living well without having to worry about making more money. Also the primary goal of this book.

G

Gifts
Items or money that one receives free of charge or expectation.

H

High Rate of Security
Low risk to the consumer.

I

Impulse Shopping
Purchasing products and/or services without doing research.

Interest Rate
There are two types of interest rates. If you are saving money, the interest rate is the amount that you will be paid (percentage of money deposited) as long as the money is in the account.

If you are borrowing money, as with a credit card, the interest rate is the amount that your account will be charged (percentage of amount borrowed) for the privilege of borrowing money.

Invention
The creation (or re-creation) of a concept or product that has never been thought of before.

K

Keystoning
Selling your product of service for twice the amount that you pay for it.

L

Leads
People that you think will purchase your product/service in the future.

Long-Term Gain
Holding your income earning shares of stock for longer than a year.

Lower Rate of Return
Greater chance that your money will not lower in value.

M

Minimum Balance
The smallest amount of money that you have to maintain in an account.

Minimum Wage
This is the minimum amount that the government demands businesses pay to employees.

N

Negotiate
Bargaining or discussing the terms of an agreement or sale.

P

Portfolio
Collection of accounts.

R

Raise
Increase in wage.

Referrals
Recommendations on your behalf.

Reinvesting
Putting money or resources back into your business (for example, education, stocks, purchasing equipment, etc.).

Repeat Business
When a customer purchases your product or service more than once.

Resources

Assets that are available for you to use.

Resume

A one-page sheet that lists your contact information, education, skill-set, and goals. This will help possible employers to gain information about you before or during an interview.

S

Sale Price

An amount determined by the seller of an item that is below the amount the item normally sells for.

Social Security

A portfolio of tax money that Americans and American companies have been paying into through payroll deductions. When someone reaches retirement age they will get money back from the portfolio for the rest of their lives.

T

Taxable Income

Money that you received in any given year that is eligible to be taxed by the government.

Taxes

Money that the government requires from its citizens to run public institutions and services.

U

Unit Cost

The price for one item.

W

Wage

An agreed upon amount of money that an employer pays an employee.

Withheld

Taken out of or removed.

HEY THERE...

Didn't find the word you wanted? Want to add a word to our list? Go to the Web site and let us know. *gotmoola.com*

Here's another **Idea Egg** for you to crack. If you haven't already done this exercise, jump back to **page 129:**

1) Your First Word

2) Three Related Words

3) Three Line Drawing

4) Your "I will" Sentence

5) Three Things You Need

6) The Thing You Can Make

7) Three Words Go Together

YOUR IDEA

IDEA EGG

My company is: _____ (see #7)

I make: _____ (see #6)

Here's another **Idea Egg** for you to crack. If you haven't already done this exercise, jump back to page 129:

1) Your First Word

2) Three Related Words

3) Three Line Drawing

4) Your "I will" Sentence

5) Three Things You Need

6) The Thing You Can Make

7) Three Words Go Together

YOUR IDEA

IDEA EGG

My company is: _____ (see #7)

I make: _____ (see #6)

Here's another **Idea Egg** for you to crack. If you haven't already done this exercise, jump back to **page 129**:

1) Your First Word

2) Three Related Words

3) Three Line Drawing

4) Your "I will" Sentence

5) Three Things You Need

6) The Thing You Can Make

7) Three Words Go Together

YOUR IDEA

IDEA EGG

My company is: _____ (see #7)

I make: _____ (see #6)

THE CAR CAPER

Read the story below and see if you can guess what kind of opportunity we are describing.

A teenage boy loves cars but doesn't think he'll ever be able to afford one, at least not for a long time. He constantly reads all about the new engines, the hybrids, fuel cels, cars designed with solar wings; all of it.

He designs cars on a pad, while his two best friends play an online racing game. They love playing games. They have even been teaching themselves how to program their own game.

The teenager announces to his friends that they can make lots of money together and have an absolute blast… and they can start right now as equal partners with the caveat that the company get a company car with the first profits… He puts his hand out and his two best friends grin and shake it.

What is the idea?

Together they'll create the coolest car game ever and charge other teens like them to play it… He can draw, they can program

TWO-MINUTE MONEY MYSTERY

THE INTERN...
Can you solve the mystery?

A teenager steps into the bank president's office to ask for a summer internship as his assistant. He smiles at her nerve and says he'll give her a chance. He points to three files on his desk. Each one is a business that he has invested in. One of them has succeeded wildly, the other two have closed. If she can pick the one that succeeded the internship is hers…

1) People love football and they love extreme sports. A tremendously successful promoter wants to join with a major TV network and do Extreme Football with star announcers and real athletes.

2) In the 1970's people sent packages via the post office with stamps or UPS. A young person with a business plan that he wrote in college wants to rent jets and deliver packages overnight, all over the country.

3) Two large companies sell the most computer operating systems. Another company, that sells millions of computers and that makes great business software decides to bring out a new operating system that would be cheaper and better.

Which one was the success?

(2) – Fed Ex is the name of that company.

159

HAVING IT ALL

Read the story below and see if you can guess what kinds of opportunity we are describing.

A fifteen year old girl's grandmother gave her $100. She told the girl that she wanted her to buy a brand new car with it when she graduated from high school. The girl laughed and asked how? The grandmother asked her what her favorite hobby was. The girl answered… Shopping. The grandmother asked her what her favorite thing was to shop for. The girl answered… cute tops. The grandmother asked her what type of tops and the girl said, ones that have cool words on them. The grandmother asked her how much she paid for the tops and the girl said twenty to forty dollars. The grandmother asked her if she could find a screen printer online or in her neighborhood and the girl said 'yes'. The grandmother asked if she had friends that liked to buy and wear the same types of clothes she did, and the girl said 'yes'. The grandmother then told her to enjoy her new car and hung up. The girl was puzzled for a moment and then smiled.

How is she going to get her car?

With her $100 the girl can buy five shirts and have them printed with cool words that she and her friends will like. She can sell them for twice as much as they cost her and then buy ten shirts and do it again, and then twenty shirts and then forty and on and on until she has enough money to buy her car.

Here's a cool way to use your money instead of spending it. During the depression, people would wear their cash so that they would always have some money on hand. For more of these, check out **gotmoola.com**

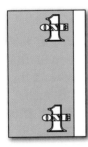

First, start with a crisp dollar bill facing with the back side up. Fold the white border at the top and bottom of the bill toward the other side. The picture here only shows one half, but do this evenly along the entire length of the bill.

Fold the bill as close to exactly in half as you can, the long way (see the diagram). Do this twice. If you've folded very carefully, the "1" insignia will

be evenly framed top and bottom, and the width will be the same all across.

On one end of the bill, fold the white border at the edge back. Fold on the other side of the "1" insignia so that it is evenly framed in a square as shown. Once you're done it should look like the diagram below.

To make the description easier in the next couple steps we'll call this end of the bill the **head**. The other end of the bill will be called the **tail**.

Now, start curving the bill away from the **head**. Pay attention to the direction of the curve relative the folds made in the head. If you curve the wrong way you won't be able to complete later steps.

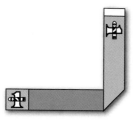

Next make a 90 degree bend in the bill. Where this bend is made will determine the size of the ring. The further from the head, the larger the ring. Once you're used to making these, you can wrap the curve around your own finger to estimate the correct position for this fold.

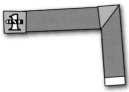

Now wrap the tail tightly around as shown. (In this diagram the **head** is shown in the same position as in the previous diagram, and the tail folds underneath.)

Using the curve created three steps above, loop the head back around to a position on top of the 90 degree bend made in the previous steps. Continue wrapping the **tail** around the body of the ring until all the excess length of the tail is used up. If you've followed the previous steps closely, the very end of the tail will be on the outside of the ring.

Using your fingernail (or anything else that works) and spread the gap between the wrapped portion of the tail and the body of the ring. In this gap, tuck the last fold in the **head**.

YOU DID IT ! **Now, wear your money proudly!**

FUNNY MONEY FACTS

Even money changes over time. In fact, in the U.S., money has quite a colorful past. Here are some tidbits that you may not know about the money you're putting into your portfolio. For more of these, check out **gotmoola.com.**

1. In 1943, because of World War II, the Lincoln penny was minted in steel and coated with zinc to save copper for the war effort.

2. A check is only good for six months from the time it is written.

3. The flag flying over the Parliament Building, on a Canadian $2 bill, is an American flag!

4. The Liberty Head Nickel, U.S. paper money was once backed by gold or, in the case of Silver Certificates, silver.

5. On an American $1 bill, look at the shield in the upper right corner of the face around the 1. There is an owl sitting on the upper left-hand corner of the shield. There is a spider hidden in the front upper right-hand corner.

6. The largest bill ever printed in U.S. currency was the $100,000 bill. It only circulated between branches of the Federal Reserve and is no longer used. See if you can find out who's on the face of one of these rare bills.

7. All 50 states are listed across the top of the Lincoln Memorial on the back of a $5 bill.

8. The Jefferson nickel replaced the Buffalo nickel in 1938. The back side is a likeness of Montecello, Jefferson's home in Charlottesville, Virginia. The design was the result of a competition and was chosen from almost 400 entries.

SWING ONLINE WITH MOOLA @
GOTMOOLA.COM

- SHARE YOUR IDEAS
- DOWNLOAD COOL GAMES
- CHECK YOUR STOCKS
- OPEN A BANK ACCOUNT
- GET BUSINESS UPDATES
- READ ABOUT OTHER KIDS

- MORE BIZWHIZ BIOS
- BIZ CARD MAKER
- BUSINESS PLAN BUILDER
- RESUME BUILDER
- MORE COOL JOB IDEAS
- FLYER MAKER & MORE !!